A. J.

ZINZENDORF
THE ECUMENICAL
PIONEER

A Study in the
Moravian Contribution to
Christian Mission and Unity

Moravian Church in America
1021 Center Street, Bethlehem, PA 18018
459 South Church Street, Winston-Salem, NC 27101

The cover sketch of Zinzendorf at age twenty is copied from a painting by Alexis Simon Belle. The original painting is in the Moravian Archives in Herrnhut, Germany.

Cover designer: Ron Tinsley

Library of Congress Catalog Card Number: 63-7179

ISBN: 1-878422-39-1

Published by
Board of Communications
Moravian Church in America
P.O. Box 1245
Bethlehem, PA 18016-1245
telephone 800-732-0591
fax 610-866-9223
e-mail <pubs@mcnp.org>

Printed in the United States of America

CONTENTS

PREFACE

In writing this book I have turned to many sources old and new, both Moravian and from other denominations. In particular I wish to acknowledge the penetrating study by Dr W. G. Addison of *The Renewed Church of the United Brethren 1722–1930*, published by the SPCK for the Church Historical Society in 1932. I am grateful to the Rev. Dr J. Alan Kay, editor of *The London Quarterly and Holborn Review*, for permission to reproduce material from my bicentenary article on Zinzendorf, April 1960.

To so many workers in the ecumenical movement I am in a deep debt for their patience, encouragement and learning. My sincerest gratitude is offered to Mrs E. Shawe, widow of the late Bishop C. H. Shawe who first introduced me to Zinzendorf; to Bishop G. W. MacLeavy and to the Rev. J. H. Foy and the Rev. L. J. Britton of the British Province of the Moravian Church; to Bishop K. G. Hamilton and Dr J. S. Groenfeldt of the American Province; and to Dr. J. M. van der Linde of the Continental Province. Perhaps I may be allowed to thank my Anglican friends through the name of Dr Norman Sykes, the late Dean of Winchester, whose knowledge of the Moravian story was profound and whose generous help to students of ecclesiastical history was so richly inspiring and renewing; and my Free Church friends through the name of the Rev. John Murray who in the busiest of lives seems to find time for everybody and everything.

To my colleague, Mr H. R. Thomas, the warmest thanks are given, and also to my students at Manchester and Newton Park who argued fiercely but with great charity about the issues raised in these pages. To my wife, Mollie, who puts up with a constant litter of papers, and to my sons, Roger and Adrian, who provide a constant litter of questions, my gratitude is renewed daily and with increasing amazement.

Bath, January 1962   A.J.L.

PROLOGUE

At any time between 1746 and 1755 you might have seen the distinguished figure of Count Zinzendorf walking swiftly through the streets of London; unlocking the gate of the College garden in Westminster, with the Dean's key, to arrive at his lodgings in College street; or coming down to the river from Lindsey House, his historic mansion in suburban Chelsea. You would notice how the people bow to him, step out of his way, or gladly render him a service. But the Count is free from all affectation. He assumes no grand or solemn airs. He is, as his first biographer called him, 'a knight of Jesus Christ'.[1] 'He is a plain man', wrote John Gambold, 'who proceeds straightforward, and, amidst all the riches of his active and extensive genius, will always be serving.'

At this time, Zinzendorf was of a middle height and inclined to corpulence. His forehead was broad and ample; his nose well shaped and slightly Roman; his lips well formed and calmly closed, and his glance quick and penetrating. His countenance was sublime and capable of great expression, but it was his eyes that summoned men to look and look again; they were dark blue, full of fire and in constant action. They were the eyes of a visionary. He was dreaming vast dreams—embracing the whole world. By the eye of faith he saw the Christian gospel carried to the farthest corners of the earth and all men everywhere joined in the fellowship of the Lamb of God. His pockets, stuffed as usual with letters from Pennsylvania, from Greenland, Surinam, South Africa, Persia and a host of other fields in the apostolate, proved that he was no idle dreamer. He dreamed in terms of action. He was creating not only a colony of Heaven, but a new spiritual commonwealth. But he sought no

---

[1] Augustus Gottlieb Spangenberg, *Life of Zinzendorf*: ET by Samuel Jackson, London 1838; original German ed. Barby, 1772–5.

throne; neither he nor the members of his Moravian Church sought anything for themselves.

In his own day, Zinzendorf was famed throughout Christendom. His name was beloved by slaves in the West Indies, Eskimos in Greenland, Indians in Pennsylvania, Hottentots in South Africa and the Negroes in Surinam. On the Continent, Bengel hailed him as 'the prophet of the age', and he has been recognized as 'certainly the greatest German Evangelical since Luther'.[1] Many Englishmen looked to him for guidance in the infant days of the Evangelical Revival. As early as March 1736, John Wesley dared 'to interrupt your more weighty matters with a letter of mine' to ask for Zinzendorf's prayers.[2] Isaac Watts revered him as 'a person of uncommon zeal and piety, and of an evangelic spirit'.[3] Philip Doddridge went to the heart of the matter when he described him as 'that blessed herald of the Redeemer'.[4] He is outstandingly relevant today, for 'what he says', as Bishop Baudert writes, 'is often as modern as if he stood among us and spoke to us as his contemporaries.'[5]

Count Nicolaus Ludwig von Zinzendorf was born in Dresden on 26 May 1700. He was a prodigious personality, prodigious in gifts, in vision and in achievement. He was a poet and hymn-writer, a pastor and teacher, a missionary, theologian, liturgist and ecclesiastical statesman, but all these offices—remarkably realized in themselves—were the outgrowth of one supreme devotion: Zinzendorf's simple, unquestioning, unyielding and all-embracing devotion to the Lamb of God and to his cause of Christian unity in all the world. 'I have but one passion,' he declared; ''tis He, 'tis only He.' 'To seek for souls, souls, in order that Jesus may receive those who love Him and that His Kingdom may be inhabited, that is my work', he wrote.[6] His all-absorbing interest, says Karl Barth, was to implement the idea of a free connexion between all

[1] A. L. Drummond, *German Protestantism since Luther* (London, 1951), pp. 72 f.
[2] *The Letters of John Wesley* (London, 1931), vol. i, p. 195.
[3] *Acta Fratrum Unitatis in Anglia* (London, 1749), p. 42.
[4] Daniel Benham, *Memoirs of James Hutton* (London, 1856), p. 60.
[5] *International Review of Missions* (July 1932), p. 392.
[6] *Ibid.* (October 1957), p. 422.

the Churches, based on their 'common love of the Saviour'.[1] Dr Norman Sykes affirms that Zinzendorf was 'in truth a pioneer of oecumenism';[2] and it is that seminal ideal which now teases the thought and increasingly inspires the vision of awakened Christians today. Since 'Edinburgh, 1910', the Ecumenical Movement has progressed along the way of dialogue into broadening plains of fellowship and hope and adventure. 'Although the passion for Christian unity is still confined to far too few', writes the Bishop of Bristol, 'there has emerged a small army of those, drawn from every part of Christendom (including Rome), who now know each other's convictions intimately and systematically.'[3] We shall see that Zinzendorf's pioneer importance in the ecumenical story lies not so much in his achievement—considerable as that was in the light of his own day—as in his exploration. Many of the acutest insights of the most modern ecumenical thinkers are found, on examination, to have been already discovered by him.

It is the grandeur of the vision of Zinzendorf, amidst the narrow confines of his own century, that first staggers us. As Dr Visser 't Hooft reports from the Moravian historian, Heinz Renkewitz, it was Zinzendorf who first used the word *Oikoumene* to carry 'the meaning: the world-wide Christian Church'.[4] Zinzendorf had a brilliant insight into the organic relationship between the missionary movement and the ecumenical movement long before 'Edinburgh, 1910' and the succeeding great conferences. Dr Visser 't Hooft has reminded us that 'the word ecumenical . . . must not be isolated from the missionary and evangelistic context in which it belongs'.[5] It is a fair claim to make for Zinzendorf that he was the first in the modern world to set the word ecumenical in that context.

No ecumenical thinker has been more aware than Zinzendorf of the scandal of disunity within Christendom due to the intractable self-will of men, but this did not lead him to condemn the existence

---

[1] *From Rousseau to Ritschl* (London, 1959), p. 44.
[2] In a broadcast, 9 May 1957.
[3] Preface to *One Lord, One Baptism* (London, 1960), p. 5.
[4] *The Meaning of Ecumenical* (London, 1953), p. 18.   [5] *Ibid.*, p. 28.

of the different denominations; rather did he welcome them as a part of 'God's economy' to body forth the rich diversity of his gifts to men. He regarded each denomination as a 'school of wisdom' with its own particular contribution to make to the whole Body of Christ. In his respect for the denominations and in his encouragement of a true denominational loyalty, Zinzendorf had long foreshadowed the splendid insight of William Temple in 1942: 'We shall impoverish our service of the wider fellowship if we let our membership of our own Communion become hesitant or indefinite. Rather we have to make strong the bonds of our own unity . . . maintaining all that we have received but recognizing also God's gifts to His people through traditions other than our own.'[1] It was an insight which led him to a deep respect for the State or National Churches. He was 'shocked' by the Methodist tendency to separate from the Church of England and he endeavoured to keep them within the pale of their 'former constitution'.[2] But Zinzendorf was under no illusion. He knew that all these visible churches had only a relative value. He strove to gather in a 'Congregation of God in the Spirit'—a commonwealth of Churches within the one Church of Christ—'the children of God who are scattered abroad' (John 11.52). In this way he hoped the Invisible Church would be made visible. He failed but his dream lives on. The conception of the *Una Sancta*, the one Church of Christ, as 'the mighty commonwealth of God, universal, holy, with a majestic history, with divine sanctions of its own superseding those of any fractional groupings', has now a wide acceptance in the ecumenical encounter.[3]

There can be no understanding of Zinzendorf nor of his ecumenical passion without the fullest appreciation of his utter devotion to the Lamb of God. He lived and witnessed under the overwhelming conviction that our ultimate unity is in Christ. It was said at a conference of Moravians in 1750 that from a child Zinzendorf 'had no other plan than to get into personal contact with the Saviour, and to obey His words like a slave, to proclaim the Person

---

[1] *The Church Looks Forward* (London, 1944), p. 4.
[2] C. W. Towlson, *Moravian and Methodist* (London, 1957), p. 173.
[3] T. Wedel, *The Coming Great Church* (London, 1947), p. 24.

of the Saviour throughout the world, not in a formal way, but in the way of the Spirit's illumination and power, and to remove everything which might hinder the coming of the Saviour to the heart'.[1] John Albertini thus described the secret at the centre of Zinzendorf's life and vision: 'It was love to Christ that glowed in the heart of the child; the same love that thrilled his middle-age; the same love that inspired his every endeavour.'[2]

Proceeding from such a first premise it was inevitable that Zinzendorf should be impatient of 'the speculating method'. As Dr Newton Flew points out, 'Zinzendorf did not break with these (dogmatic) formularies, but he laid all the stress on the religious experience which those formularies should explain and guard'.[3] He once declared that 'all the essential theology can be written with large characters on one octavo sheet'. The *odium theologicum*, which in his day as in our own provided perhaps the greatest single obstacle to Christian unity, Zinzendorf detested like the plague. His ecumenical theology arose from the religious experience of those who 'have experienced the Death of Jesus on their hearts'.[4] It was a *Herzens-religion* that he preached: without it, all efforts towards unity he regarded as unfounded and doomed. A modern ecumenical theologian underlines Zinzendorf's insight in this matter and quotes his warning: 'All fellowship (*gemeinschaft*) which is only based on agreement of opinions and forms without a change of heart, is a dangerous sect.'[5]

[1] Quoted by W. G. Addison, *The Renewed Church of the United Brethren* (London, 1932), p. 20.

[2] J. E. Hutton, *A History of the Moravian Church* (London, 1909), p. 398.

[3] *The Idea of Perfection* (London, 1934), p. 343. Dr Flew goes on to indicate Zinzendorf's importance in a field which we cannot pursue here: 'Ritschl correctly describes the introduction of this method of regarding dogmatic formularies as an epoch in evangelical Christianity, because not only was Lutheranism influenced through Zinzendorf and Schleiermacher, but the origin of Methodism was due to the application of the same method. It is a further reflection that in his appeal to sentiment and to the direct experience of the individual, Zinzendorf was a forerunner of Goethe and the Romanticists'. *Ibid.*, pp. 343–4.

[4] See Zinzendorf's *Maxims* (ed. John Gambold, London, 1751), pp. 256–7.

[5] W. A. Visser 't Hooft, *The Pressure of our Common Calling* (London, 1959), p. 27.

It was in God's good providence that Zinzendorf was introduced at the right hour to the descendants of the ancient Unitas Fratrum, the Unity of the Brethren, known also to history as the Moravian Church. Their ecumenical traditions were so germane to his own religious insights that he was able to respond to them instinctively and by his own gifts of genius to quicken their application to the fields of practical Christianity across the world. Indeed the life of Zinzendorf became so inextricably bound up with the renewed Moravian Church that a study of his ecumenical witness cannot be separated from a consideration of that Church. But within the scope of this book, such a consideration can only be incidental to the portrayal of Zinzendorf's own ideas and achievements.

For the Unitas Fratrum the whole relevance of Christianity was an adventure in partnership or fellowship (*koinonia*) with all the children of God in every place and every congregation who would respond. The *koinonia* was primary. It began with Christ and in it everything was orientated towards Christ and participated in him. From thereon the only possibility was to think and act centrifugally.[1] This legacy from the Unitas Fratrum deepened for Zinzendorf his own conception of that unity with Christ and with our fellow Christians which was to be comparable with Christ's own union with the Father: 'That they may be one as we are one' (John 17.11). The accents of this deepest unity—beyond any agreement in doctrine, ritual and order—which Zinzendorf sought to spread and make manifest to the world in the Moravian apostolate, have been admirably caught in a statement by Bishop Lesslie Newbigin: 'The unity which we must seek is thus a unity which arises from Christ's indwelling in his people, and from their being in him. It is not simply a unity of organization nor is it simply an agreement about doctrine. It is a total mutual interchange of being —Christ wholly given to us, we wholly given to him. . . . Its character is most simply described by saying that those participate in it who love one another as Christ loved them.'[2] Zinzendorf called

[1] J. M. van der Linde, 'The Moravian Church' in *International Review of Missions*, October, 1957, p. 422.

[2] Quoted by Dr Visser 't Hooft, *op. cit.*, p. 90.

this unity a 'Marriage of Souls' forming the very 'Diocese or Flock of the Lamb Himself'.[1]

Such a unity, said Zinzendorf, must be seen to be in the world. It must be made manifest here and now although its full manifestation belongs to the final consummation. It was the glorious task of the Unitas Fratrum, as renewed in the Moravian Church, to 'exist as an example' of such unity, bearing more and more 'the signature of a congregation and people of Christ', seeking a qualitative and not a quantitative character, serving the cause of unity in all the denominations, and then being ready and willing to disappear from the scene.[2] Certainly no communion of Christians can ever have displayed this unity more convincingly and fruitfully than the Moravian Brethren in the time of Zinzendorf. More than a hundred Bachelors of Divinity, Lectors, Masters and Students of the University of Jena wrote to the Moravians at Herrnhut, 17 August 1728: 'Praise ye the Lord with us, who has united our dispersed Members thro' a Living Power; to which we have been mostly moved by the glorious instance of your intimate love and union.'[3] 'They live together in perfect love and peace', was the verdict of the Yorkshire clergyman, Benjamin Ingham, upon the Moravians.[4] John Wesley, amongst the Moravians in Germany, wrote to his brother Samuel: 'I am with a Church whose conversation is in heaven. . . . As they have all one Lord and one faith, so they are all partakers of one Spirit, the spirit of meekness and love, which uniformly and continually animates all their conversation.'[5]

Zinzendorf loved the Moravians and their irenic spirit. 'I judge the Church of the Brethren', he wrote, 'to be the only Church under Heaven which can be said to be truly unprejudiced against her Fellow Sisters, never taking any part in their Quarrels, never

---

[1] *Maxims*, p. 240.
[2] See Addison, *op. cit.*, p. 146, for a most interesting Anglican statement of the same position.
[3] *Acta Fratrum*, p. 22.
[4] L. Tyerman, *Oxford Methodists* (London, 1873), p. 68.
[5] *Letters*, vol. i, pp. 250–1.

judging any Body, or its Members, remaining without her Pale.'[1]
It was he who directed the Moravian ecumenical witness and who
expressed their spirit, as in this hymn:

> Christian hearts, in love united,
>   Seek alone in Jesus rest;
> Has he not your love excited?
>   Then let love inspire each breast;
> Members—on our Head depending,
>   Light—reflecting him our Sun,
> Brethren—his commands attending,
>   We in him, our Lord, are one.
>
> Come then, come, O flock of Jesus,
>   Covenant with him anew;
> Unto him, who conquered for us,
>   Pledge we love and service true;
> And should our love's union holy
>   Firmly linked no more remain,
> Wait ye at his footstool lowly,
>   Till he draw it close again.
>
> Grant, Lord, that with thy direction,
>   'Love each other', we comply,
> Aiming with unfeigned affection
>   Thy love to exemplify;
> Let our mutual love be glowing;
>   Thus will all men plainly see,
> That we, as on one stem growing,
>   Living branches are in thee.
>
> O that such may be our union,
>   As thine with the Father is,
> And not one of our communion
>   E'er forsake the path of bliss;

[1] *An Exposition* or True State of the matters objected in England to the
People known by the name of Unitas Fratrum (London, 1755), pt. i, p. 58.

> May our light 'fore men with brightness,
> From thy light reflected, shine;
> Thus the world will bear us witness,
> That we, Lord, are truly thine.[1]

It would be idle to pretend that Zinzendorf was without fault—his temper seems to have greatly resembled that of Luther—but no man's life could have been more of an *eirenicon*. 'Whatever he did and said', wrote Spangenberg, 'testified of his tender love to the Saviour and the members of that church, which He has so dearly purchased.' He devoted particular attention, said Spangenberg, to those that were weak, simple, ungifted, and thus—according to the usual mode of thinking—worthless and despicable; and, if he perceived in them a love to the Saviour, they were much esteemed by him.[2]

It was in Zinzendorf's unsullied tolerance and uncommon tenderness, in an age of 'high church walls', for all sorts of souls of what persuasion soever, that his irenic spirit is most clearly to be seen. He made it a rule, for example, that once a year, on the Great Day of Atonement, the Moravian Church should pray for the conversion of Israel. On a voyage to the West Indies, he discovered a poor Jewish family in the steerage, the wife very sick. He turned over his cabin to her while he spent the rest of the voyage below in the ill smelling part of the ship. He would enter into no polemic against the Church of Rome—and that in an age of much Protestant bigotry and jealousy. He wrote:

I have been severely censured for not acknowledging the Pope to be *the Antichrist*, as I am sure he is not, and cannot be deemed so upon the authority of the Bible. I never spoke upon that topic, but when called upon in lands, where he is abused for fashion sake. . . . Moreover, if the Church of Rome deviates from the Letter of the Gospel, which I am satisfied she will not deny; I could wish, when some Protestants, doing the very same, deny it afterwards, they might not appear liars before God. In short, every Church bearing

[1] *Moravian Hymn Book* (London, 1912), No 512.
[2] *Zinzendorf*, p. 509.

19

the name of Christ, and confessing him to be the Creator and Redeemer of the World, and her Chief in Reality (whatever courtesy may be paid to men) I take her to be a Congregation formed for his sake; more or less erroneous, more or less dissolute, more or less liable to correction, punishment or destruction. But in the meantime, I respect her rulers, I suffer not my people to disturb her directly or indirectly, if I can help it; I protest against it, as against an abuse; I love her members as brethren; and tho' I thank my Saviour for my nearness to himself, I never will boast of it and despise others.[1]

[1] *An Exposition*, pt. i, p. 50.

I

THE YOUNG PIETIST

The Influence of Pietism

ZINZENDORF was cradled in religion. He was descended from one of the most ancient noble families in the Archduchy of Austria, and his paternal grandfather had emigrated for conscience' sake after the abolition of Protestant liberty in his native land. George Ludwig, the father of Zinzendorf, had gone into Saxony where he became a Minister of State. He was a personal friend of Philip Jacob Spener, the leader of the movement known as Pietism, and was himself a man full of faith. He died when his son was only six weeks old, and his last words to him had the aura of prophecy about them: 'My dear son, they ask me to bless you, but you are more blessed than I am; though even now I feel as if I were already standing before the throne of Jesus.'

After his mother's second marriage, little 'Lutz', as Zinzendorf was called, was taken by his grandmother, the Baroness Catherine von Gersdorf, and his aunt Henrietta, to live in their castle at Gross-Hennersdorf in Upper Lusatia, once a hunting lodge of the Bohemian kings.

The castle was a home of Pietism. The Baroness was an evangelical scholar of some repute, learned in theology and in the Greek and Hebrew languages. She maintained a wide contact and an extensive correspondence with the religious leaders in the Church, at Court and in the Universities. The eminent Pietists often visited her and she endeavoured to carry out their principles in her own family. By holding numerous meetings on her estates she sought to awaken her dependants to a personal and practical devotion to Jesus Christ. Amid such surroundings, Zinzendorf's education was exclusively Pietistic, under Pietist tutors, and although his health was not robust, he proved a brilliant and willing pupil. He was, as Monsignor Knox rightly observed, one of those persons 'who seem made for religion'.[1]

What, then, was Pietism? A Protestant Scholasticism had arisen in Germany. By the middle of the seventeenth century the rich warm life of the Reformation had gone to sleep in the cold dogmatic slumber of the Lutheran Church. The Pietist movement was a call to action; a call to vigorous Christian experience out-feeling the passive acceptance of creed and conformity; a call to all those who 'meant the word in earnest' to meet together to stir the Church— and hence the world—to a living Christian discipleship, to true piety, to works of mercy and evangelism. It arose in Saxony and the name 'Pietist' was first used, as a term of ridicule, at Frankfurt-on-Main in 1674. The founder, Spener, published his ideas in the *Pia Desideria* of 1675. He organized little gatherings or 'meetings of piety' (*collegia pietatis*) among his hearers in Frankfurt and later in Berlin where the Elector Frederick William III of Brandenburg befriended him. In 1694 the Elector established a University at Halle which supported the Pietists against the University of Wittenberg and its allegations that Spener was guilty of 264 errors. Spener's friend, August Hermann Francke, was appointed to the University of Halle and in that city he founded institutions which were to become famous all over Germany as the training-ground of Pietist students and pastors.

Sometime before Francke's death in 1727, Pietism had gone adrift into a spirit of punctilious and pharisaic legalism, and Zinzendorf was to outgrow and rebel against its more rigid principles. But at the time of Spener's and Francke's visits to Gross-Hennersdorf, the movement was still in its baptismal purity and alive with men whose hearts God had touched.

From all the conversations at the castle and from the instructions of his tutors, first at Gross-Hennersdorf and then at Francke's Paedagogium in Halle, Zinzendorf discovered in detail the ideals of

[1] R. A. Knox, *Enthusiasm, A Chapter in the History of Religion* (Oxford, 1950), p. 399.

the Pietists and the means whereby they sought to awaken the people, inside and outside the Church, to that same sense of personal devotion and service to Jesus Christ which he himself seemed to have received so early in life as a gift from God. The Pietists preached the religion of the *heart*, and sought to emphasize in all the Confessions that which would unite the followers of Christ in a common practical discipleship; one drop of love, they declared, was worth more than a sea of knowledge. Conversion was the touchstone of Christianity for them: they divided men not into orthodox and heretic, but into converted and unconverted. The Pietists perpetually laid down the path to sanctification. The earnest Christian must deny himself the worldly pleasures such as the theatre, cards and dancing. He must meet with like-minded seekers, from any of the Churches, in the *collegia pietatis* to increase their spiritual fellowship in prayer, Bible-reading, meditation, family worship and religious conversations. By their schools, their catechisms, and by the private meetings of the congregations in which the members freely questioned the pastor on biblical matters, the Pietists carried forward their mission of Christian education.

As we have said, Zinzendorf was a brilliant pupil. He had a lively imagination and a gift for poetry; his mind was fertile and receptive; he had a command of words, a civilized irony, and he came to be well versed in the French, Greek and Latin tongues. But these things were not his primary interest. From the earliest years, Zinzendorf enjoyed an intimate and entirely natural companionship with Jesus Christ. 'I have had the happiness', he said in one of his *Discourses to Children*, 'of knowing the Saviour by experience from my youngest years. It was at Hennersdorf when I was a child that I learnt to love Him. In this way I have known the Saviour for many years; and I have carried on a friendship with Him, quite in a childlike way, sometimes talking with Him for whole hours, as we talk with a friend, going in and out of the room quite lost in my meditations. I have enjoyed this close personal intercourse with Jesus for fifty years, and I feel the happiness of it more and more every day I live.'[1]

[1] F. Bovet, *The Banished Count* (E. T. J. Gill, London, 1865), p. 16.

Even as a young child, 'I was as certain', says Zinzendorf, 'that the Son of God was my Lord as the existence of my five fingers.'[1] Little 'Lutz' would throw letters to Jesus from the castle windows; he preached sermons to his friends, and even to the chairs when no other congregation could be found; he held his own little prayer-meetings and on one occasion a detachment of Swedish soldiers, coming to demand supplies from the castle in 1706, were so overwhelmed by the earnestness of the young child at his devotions that they went quietly away. At the age of eight, the subtleties of atheism unfolded themselves in the boy's soul; but, he tells us, 'my heart clung to Jesus'. Before he was ten he had determined to be a preacher of the Gospel, and this determination 'to proclaim the Person of the Saviour throughout the world' remained his life-long purpose.

At Gross-Hennersdorf and at Halle, Zinzendorf was captivated by two cognate conceptions of Pietism which, after he had quickened them himself, were to irradiate his work for Christian unity: the conception of missions, and the conception of *ecclesiolae in Ecclesia* (little churches within the Church).

It was Leibnitz's missionary treatise, *Novissima Linica*, that stirred Francke to the Church's prime responsibility of carrying the Gospel across the seas; and when Frederick IV of Denmark asked him to support a Mission to the East Indies, he responded immediately. Three students of Halle—Ziegenbalg, Plutschau and Grundler—established a station at Tranquebar in 1706. Letters describing the work of the Mission were circulated in Europe and naturally enough they reached the Lady Gersdorf and her drawing-room meetings. Long afterwards in August 1753, Zinzendorf told a congregation of English Moravians at Fetter Lane in London how the first seed of missionary zeal was planted in him. 'I know the day, the hour, the spot in Hennersdorf,' he said; 'it was in the Great Room; the year was 1708 or 1709; I heard items read out of the paper about the East Indies, before regular reports were issued; and there and then the first mission-

---

[1] J. E. Hutton, *A History of the Moravian Church* (London, 1909), p. 179.

ary impulse arose in my soul.'[1] And in Francke's house at Halle, the young Pietist records, 'I had chances every day to hear edifying reports about the spread of the Kingdom of God, to speak with witnesses from foreign lands, and to see martyrs and prisoners; and all this strengthened my zeal for the cause of Christ'. In 1715 Zinzendorf dined many times at Francke's table and talked with the three Halle missionaries, home on furlough from Tranquebar.

Neither Spener nor Francke had any desire to separate from the Lutheran Church. Their purpose was to quicken the spiritual fellowship of the awakened Christians by developing the *collegia pietatis* into associations of believing souls who, without any formal ecclesiastical existence of their own, might exhibit a true pattern of Christ's 'flock, family and husbandry'. Such associations (*ecclesiolae*), remaining within the Church (*Ecclesia*), would serve to awaken her from 'unregenerate slumber'.

The Student Years

In a remarkable venture of the practical imagination, the young Zinzendorf attempted in the Halle Paedagogium to express both the missionary and the ecumenical conceptions. The years which he spent at Halle, 1710–16, were not happy years. His personal character was an open reproach to the moral laxity in the Paedagogium; nor did his dignity of birth and uncommon gifts increase his popularity with the masters or the boys. But they were quickening years: Zinzendorf became intensely aware of the ecumenical truth which lay at the heart of his own communion with Christ. Just as Christ was the bond of unity in his own life, so was Christ the bond of his unity with all Christians. In Christ all men are one. No peculiarity of creed or organization need separate those who call upon Christ as their Lord and Saviour. The fundamental insight became clearer: Christianity is fellowship with Christ, and through him, with all men; without such fellowship there can be no Christianity. To spread this unifying and reconciling conception of fellowship in Christ became increasingly Zinzendorf's

---

[1] J. E. Hutton, *A History of Moravian Missions*, p. 4.

consuming desire, and he lost no time in beginning his apostleship of unity.

With five other schoolboys he now formed the Order of the Grain of Mustard Seed. It was a kind of spiritual knighthood in which the flower of chivalry bound themselves to confess their Saviour in word and deed; to be a leaven among all Christians; to labour for the salvation and fellowship of all men, regardless of their own particular church connexions; to succour all those who are persecuted for their faith; and to carry the Gospel to the heathen beyond the seas. The first article of the Order affirmed that 'the members of our society will love the whole human family'. The members wore a ring with the Greek inscription: 'No man liveth unto himself'. The emblem of the Order was a gold medallion: on one side was an *ecce homo* with the inscription *vulnera Christi*, the wounds of Christ; and on the other side was an angel and the inscription *nostra medela*, our healing. Zinzendorf was the Grand Master of the Order and he wore a golden cross with an oval green front in the centre of which was a Mustard Tree. 'God knows that I never sought my glory,' Zinzendorf wrote; 'on the contrary I well knew that I should only be ridiculed.' And ridiculed he was: but in the service of Christ, Zinzendorf was always 'braver than the heavens are high'.

This embryo ecumenical fellowship spread, and in the course of years eminent churchmen and statesmen of manifold origin became members of the Order, maintaining their bond by visits and frequent correspondence. There was President von Reichenbach; Bishop Daniel Ernst Jablonski; General Oglethorpe, Governor of Georgia; Thomas Wilson, Bishop of Sodor and Man; John Potter, Archbishop of Canterbury; Cardinal de Noailles of Paris; Erskine, Secretary of State for Scotland, and King Christian VI of Denmark— an ecumenical *ecclesiola* indeed! Francke spoke the simple truth when Zinzendorf left Halle for the University of Wittenberg: 'This youth will some day become a great light in the world.'

This youth wished to pursue his theological studies, but his guardian, Count Otto Christian, had other ideas for him. First, he thought that Zinzendorf should rid himself of the taint of Pietism;

and second, that as a Count of the Empire—the highest rank of Counts in the German aristocracy—he should devote himself to the service of the State. Both these purposes might be served if the young nobleman went to Wittenberg, the seat of orthodox Lutheranism. Accordingly in September 1716 Zinzendorf proceeded to the University to study law and prepare himself for a diplomatic career.

Again his lot was not a happy one. The Pietists were scandalized because he had gone to the centre of Orthodoxy; and the divines at Wittenberg regarded him with some suspicion. But with the buoyancy of youth and an insatiable curiosity, Zinzendorf went on his way, studying the law, learned the arts of riding, fencing and dancing, and filling every spare moment with feasts of Christian history and theology. He regarded his dancing lessons as 'exercises in patience'. He was never plagued by morbid and extreme Pietistic anxiety concerning the state of his own soul; but in his early days at Wittenberg, driven back more and more upon his own inner resources, he drew near to the life of what he called 'the rigid Pietist'. He spent whole nights in prayer and meditation, fasting one day a week, and studying the Bible like a man who was never going to see it again. Wesley's Holy Club could not have exceeded him in 'Method'. But the breadth of his sympathies and his own natural tolerance delivered him.

As his acquaintance with the Wittenberg divines developed, Zinzendorf discovered that the Pietists and the orthodox Lutherans shared a common ground. It was the common ground he was to discover in all the Denominations, and he called it the Christianity of the heart. This became a fundamental conception in Zinzendorf's world-view of religion; it was to possess him all his life and drive him on to his life's task of 'reuniting the Christianities'. He discovered that this Christianity of the heart—this heart-to-heart or personal and intimate devotion to Jesus Christ and to all who acknowledged him as Saviour—rose above all the barriers of creed, forms of worship and ecclesiastical organization; it was instantly recognized by all men in every place who shared in it; and it was the meeting-ground of all Christians and of all the Churches.

Once an idea gripped Zinzendorf's attention he was seldom long in relating it to action. At the age of eighteen he determined to reconcile the Lutherans of his University to the Pietists of Halle. By 1718 he had won a wide respect in Wittenberg. 'In company', writes Spangenberg of this period in Zinzendorf's life, 'he was cheerful—in his studies diligent—in public speaking, expert—in disputing, acute—and in conduct, polite. His deportment possessed something attractive, his person something noble, and all this drew upon him the attention of everyone.'[1] Francke of Halle and Dr Wernsdorf of Wittenberg were ready to accept the young student's mediation, but when his mother objected to his meddling in such weighty matters, the project of reconciliation had to be abandoned. But already Zinzendorf's stature had been recognized, and the work of unity begun.

In the spring of 1719, at the wish of his family, Zinzendorf set out on the Grand Tour, without which the education of a young nobleman in the eighteenth century could not be regarded as complete. He went ostensibly to further his legal studies, to see the world, and to acquire the formal polish and manners of a courtier in Paris. But his driving interest was to widen his acquaintance with the varying religious traditions in Europe. His rank and character, his originality and vivacity, opened the doors of palaces and the studies of the most eminent theologians. Always a prolific writer, he recorded everything in his diary, and expressed his deepest sentiments in a stream of religious verse. He met the leaders of the Reformed (Calvinist) Church in Holland, and the Roman Catholic hierarchy in Paris. He talked with Lutherans, Pietists, Mystics and Socinians. The more he saw of these different Christianities, the more he was convinced that the Christianity of the heart was their fundamental bond of unity. And the ecumenical vision grew stronger each day within him.

In the Art Gallery at Dusseldorf, Zinzendorf stood beneath the masterly *Ecce Homo* of Domenico Feti with its crown of thorns and words of challenge: 'All this I did for thee; what doest thou for Me?' There and then the young Count asked the crucified Christ to draw him into 'the fellowship of his sufferings' and to open

[1] *Op. cit.*, pp. 11–12.

up a life of service to him. But how and where could he serve his Lord?[1]

In May 1719 Zinzendorf reached Utrecht where he studied law at the University, learned English and acquired the rudiments of medicine. The most eminent in Church and State received him, including the Prince of Orange and the famous theologian, James Basnage: 'I was glad to become acquainted with this great man,' the traveller wrote, 'he recognized the truth even in the opposite party.' In September Zinzendorf arrived in Paris, where again the highest society welcomed him. The Regent and the Dowager Duchess gave him a flattering reception at the Court. In the mornings he attended to business; in the afternoons he studied law and the French language; and the evenings he spent in society. He was something of a phenomenon at the French Court. 'People did not know what category to put me in,' he commented; 'I did not dance at the Court, and did not gamble . . . those who thought ill of me took me for a Pietist, and the Pietists would not own me.'[2] He was reputed to know the Bible by heart. 'Everybody says so,' the Dowager Duchess told him.[3]

Zinzendorf was disgusted by the artifice of the courtiers and by the pomp and vice of many of the French clergy, but this did not make his stay in Paris unfruitful. He met with some sincerely religious persons, and he became acquainted with 'some ladies who were subjects of the divine grace'. Still more he was delighted to trace among the Catholics of France something of that same spirit of tolerance which he had already found among the Protestants in Holland. In particular he made friends with Cardinal de Noailles, the Archbishop of Paris. The Cardinal attempted to win his young friend to the Roman allegiance, but seeing the futility of this, he left religious discussion and 'plunged with me into the unfathomable ocean of the sufferings and merits of Jesus'. That a young Pietist and a Catholic prelate could share this common fellowship was a transforming discovery for Zinzendorf; they differed it is true, but they esteemed each other as believers; and as the Count

[1] J. E. Hutton, *A History of the Moravian Church*, p. 186.
[2] See Spangenberg, *Zinzendorf*, p. 19.   [3] Hutton, p. 187.

wrote to the Cardinal, they could 'reunite in the wounds of our Saviour'.[1]

It would not be fair to the full character of Zinzendorf to omit a certain incident during his stay in Paris and of which he himself spoke later. 'He relates', Spangenberg tells us, 'that on one occasion he had not been received with due distinction at Court, and complained on that account to the court chamberlain, of the master of ceremonies, and requested satisfaction, which was immediately promised him. But soon after, on maturely weighing the circumstance, he found that his pride was not yet dead. On this he threw himself at the Lord's feet, besought his grace and forgiveness with many tears, and gladly gave up his rights.'[2]

In the spring of 1720, Zinzendorf left Paris. He made his way home through Switzerland. At Basle he had conversations with the outstanding theologian of the Reformed Church, Samuel Werenfels. At Castell he fell ill and stayed for a time with his aunt, the Countess, and her daughter Theodora. He became very attached to his cousin and their marriage was freely spoken of. But when he learned that his friend, Count Reuss, had been in love with Theodora for some years, he responded in a manner which to others might seem quixotic, but was in fact the natural expression of his belief that God's will must be sought and carried out in every situation. He advised Reuss to propose to Theodora and he himself did everything he could to smooth out the difficulties. Reuss and Theodora were soon married and Zinzendorf wrote a Cantata for the wedding. He told Charles Wesley, many years later, that it was a decisive moment in his life when he decided, if it was the will of God, to give up his claim to Theodora. 'From that moment I was freed from all self-seeking. My own will is hell to me.'[3]

At the Court in Dresden

Just before he came of age on 26 May 1721, Zinzendorf arrived back at Gross-Hennersdorf, a cultivated and cosmopolitan figure.

---

[1] Addison, *op. cit.*, p. 26. [2] *Zinzendorf*, p. 22.
[3] F. Bovet, *The Banished Count*, p. 55.

The Grand Tour had widened his horizons and confirmed more than ever his life's mission. He wished to enter the ministry of the State Church and work for the recognition of the principle— almost a heresy in his day—that all are members of Christ and all are brethren, whether belonging to Rome, to Wittenberg or to Jerusalem. Already Francke had invited him to share in the work at the Halle orphanage, but in deference to his family's wish that he should become a diplomat, he had refused the invitation. To enter the formal ministry of the Church was beneath the dignity of a noble, or so his family again advised him. In October 1721 Zinzendorf went to Dresden and took up the office of a King's Councillor at the Court of Augustus the Strong, King of Saxony.

Zinzendorf carried out his state duties faithfully, but his dominant mission was not forgotten. His real element was in preaching the Gospel and spreading the fellowship of all men in Jesus Christ. To the amusement of many of the aristocracy, he held an open religious meeting at his Dresden home every Sunday from three in the afternoon to seven in the evening. The congregation was drawn from every rank of society and from every stage of belief; the sceptics were welcomed if they were in earnest. They sang together, read the New Testament, and conversed freely on all aspects of religious life and thought. Once a week, Zinzendorf published a half-philosophical and half-religious paper called the *Dresden Socrates* in which he attacked the immorality and the conceits of courtiers and men-about-town. He continued to pour out a stream of religious verse and hymns. The Pietists condemned the catholicity of his interests; the courtiers found his moral satire too incisive; but his acquaintance was sought by a whole company of people who did not attend church but were in earnest in seeking the truth.

But Zinzendorf sought to do more for his Saviour. And a wider sphere of service was soon to open. In April 1722 he bought the estate of Berthelsdorf from his grandmother, and there he planned 'to plant a pleasant garden of the Lord'. He appointed John Andrew Rothe to be the minister of the Lutheran church on his estate; he welcomed the support of Frederick von Watteville, an old acquaintance of the Halle days; and Pastor Schäfer of Görlitz gladly gave his advice and support. Above all, Zinzendorf prayed that Berthelsdorf might become a place of refuge for oppressed and persecuted Christians of every kind and denomination. He had not long to wait.

2

THE UNITY OF THE BRETHREN

The Hidden Seed in Moravia

IN the spring of 1717 a young carpenter came preaching into the Moravian village of Sehlen. The Jesuits' spies were out and every Protestant went in danger, but Christian David could not be intimidated. 'This bush-preacher', wrote one of his contemporaries, 'laboured for souls beyond what words can tell.'

Christian David was born into a Catholic family in 1690. He had little education but, on the hills as a shepherd boy, he thought long and deeply about religion. In his devotions, he tells us, he 'crept on his knees round the image of the blessed Virgin' until his whole body burned like an oven. But he could find no rest to his soul. When he chanced to hear a band of Protestants praying and singing in their prison, he longed for such a faith as theirs. At the age of twenty he learned to read the Bible and to suspect Catholicism of gross error. He resolved to join the Lutherans in Hungary, but the Jesuits pursued him. After a short period in the army, he followed the trade of a carpenter and arrived in Gorlitz in Upper Lusatia. And there he was converted through the ministry of a Pietist pastor, Melchior Schafer. For twenty weeks, David was so ill that he could lift neither hand nor foot. 'Pastor Schafer came to me every day', he wrote, 'and from him it was that the gospel of Christ came first to me with power. Here I found peace I had long sought in vain, for I was assured that my sins were forgiven.'[1] Elusive as the wind, Christian David crossed and recrossed the border between Upper Lusatia and Moravia; he appeared in the mountain and forest paths,

---

[1] F. F. Hagen, *Old Landmarks* (Bethlehem, Pa., 1886), p. 130.

in the valleys and by the streams; he proclaimed the 'assurance of faith' and none who heard him would play the informer for the Jesuits.

The Neisser household welcomed the visits of the carpenter David to Sehlen. For many years they had suffered under the Catholic tyranny and they longed to escape from it. They begged the bush-preacher to find a place of refuge for them in another land where they might read the word of God and worship him in freedom.

In conversation after conversation, in the moonlit woods or in some secluded barn, Christian David heard the story of the Neissers and of their fellowship in the 'Hidden Seed'. This Hidden Seed or Remnant, he learned, was scattered over the face of Bohemia and Moravia. They looked expectantly for the revival of their Protestant fellowship. Despite the vigilant oppression under which they lived, several prophetic voices had assured them that the time of deliverance was at hand. The brave old George Jaeschke, grandfather to the Neissers, had declared in 1707, a little before he died: 'It is true, our liberty is taken from us; and it even has the appearance as though the cause of the Brethren was ruined for ever. But you, my dear children, will live to see a day of deliverance for the remnant that is left. I almost think, that you will have to emigrate into another country, where the Lord will prepare you a place, where you may serve him without fear, according to his holy word. When that time arrives, then be you ready, and take care, that you be not among the last, or remain at home. Remember, what I have told you.'[1] Such was the spirit in the Hidden Seed of the ancient Church of the Unitas Fratrum.

Unitas Fratrum: Origins

Against a background of almost constant suffering and persecution, the Unitas Fratrum had taken an historic role in the birth and growth of the Reformation.

[1] John Holmes, *History of the Protestant Church of the United Brethren* (London, 1825), vol. i, p. 153.

It began in the early months of 1457 when Gregory, called the Patriarch, led his small company of peasants, farmers, nobles, scholars and priests out of Prague and into the sheltered valley of Kunwald, one hundred miles distant and in the north-east of Bohemia. This pilgrim band of the Hussite tradition had come to Kunwald to secure that peace and freedom in which, under the headship of Christ and the standard of the Bible, they might worship according to their conscience, and share unhindered fellowship with kindred souls. They had laid bare the superstition and profligacy of the Roman Church, but their chief protest was against the Papal and priestly denial of the 'Crown Rights of the Redeemer' and of the individual believer's direct access to Christ and the benefits of his passion.

For these men and their families 'Christ was the whole of the Doctrine' and fellowship with him was the ground-spring of the whole Christian life. Starting from the given unity in Christ, these men of Kunwald were to inspire their descendants to carry the fellowship of Christ and his Gospel to the remotest recesses of the inhabited earth. The logic of this 'reaching out'—as the process of history afforded opportunity—was inevitable. Redeemed and made strong in the fellowship of Jesus Christ, the individual soul needs must reach out to its neighbour, congregation to congregation, province to province, and church to church. And it is this seed of ecumenicity that led Gregory and his pilgrim band to call themselves 'brethren' and 'sisters' and that inspired them to found the *Jednota Bratrska*, in Latin *Unitas Fratrum*, in English the Unity of the Brethren, on 1 March 1457.

From the beginning, the unhindered fellowship of Christ secured a spiritual democracy in the Unity of the Brethren. A godly priest, named Michael Bradacius, ministered to the Brethren, and as he handed them all—laity and ordained alike—the cup at the Lord's Supper, this spiritual democracy was symbolized and affirmed. In the Roman Catholic Church, the cup had been denied to the laity; but the Brethren now asserted, by this simple act of Michael Bradacius, that all men were equal before God and had equal freedom of access to him. In all Bohemia, the cup was to become the symbol on buildings, books and banners, of the claim for equal rights of all believers before God and the Church.

But intent as they were on securing the individual's fellowship with Christ, the Brethren were also intensely aware that this fellowship could not survive in isolation: it must be worked out in the fellowship of the congregation. The congregation's community, the unity of brethren and sisters in Christ, necessarily flowed to and from the individual's living unity in Christ. This truth was affirmed in a characteristic statement at the first Synod of the Unitas Fratrum, held in the mountains of Reichenau, 1464:

> In the Congregations we will preserve peace with all, cultivate brotherly harmony, and do all in our power to further the common well-being, and to maintain firmly the bond of brotherhood in and with and through God.[1]

The Brethren agreed to observe Christian obedience, acknowledge their faults and shortcomings before God and man, and to accept instruction, warning, exhortation and reproof from one another in the spirit of brotherly good will. If any brother should prove unfaithful to the covenant of fellowship made with Christ and the community of believers, then, after due process, it would be necessary 'to exclude him from the fellowship'. Step by step the foundations were laid of that Discipline which, continued and modified from the Statutes of Reichenau (1464), the *Ratio Disciplinae* (1616) to the Brotherly Agreement of the eighteenth century, was to be the envy of the other Christian communions.[2]

It cannot be emphasized too much that the community at Kunwald did not regard itself as a splinter or break-away movement. The Brethren held too precious the 'seamless robe of Christ', ever to think lightly of setting up another branch of the Church of

---

[1] D. Benham, *Origin and Episcopate of the Bohemian Brethren* (London, 1867), p. 43. Benham gives the Statutes agreed upon by the Brethren at Reichenau, pp. 38–44.

[2] Full details of the organization of the fellowship at all levels in the ancient Unitas Fratrum can be found in the *Ratio Disciplinae Ordinisque Ecclesiastici in Unitate Fratrum Bohemorum*, issued by order of the Synod of Zerawic, April 1616. Bishop Seifferth produced a Latin-English edition of this work in London, 1866.

Christendom. Down to 1467 theirs was still a reforming movement within the Roman Catholic Church, intent to purge away the gross corruption and superstition, and to offer fellowship to all men of like aspiration. And the little community continued to grow. News of its formation ran like wild-fire through the underground channels of reform in Bohemia and Moravia. 'At that time', wrote Jaffet, 'friend longed for friend, brother for brother, so that more persons continually joined the Brethren.'

But already by 1461 the pattern of persecution and exile which was to run through most of the history of the Unitas Fratrum had revealed itself. The Roman Church cried 'heresy', and the State cried 'treason', and both combined to crush the Brethren. Gregory was put to the rack; some of the Brethren were mutilated; some burned to death; many of them languished in prison; Kunwald and the other meeting-places were broken up and the members driven from their homes in the depth of winter. A number of the flock contrived to escape to the mountains and forests surrounding Brandeis. Because they were forced to live in the caves and the holes of the earth, their enemies nicknamed them the 'Pitmen'. But as the night-fires gleamed the refugees read the Bible, sang their hymns, planned for the future and rejoiced together in the fellowship of Christ and his sufferings. In the autumn of 1463, the Bishop of Breslau advised the King of Bohemia that the Brethren's martyrdom was 'apt to breed maggots'; and the persecution ceased. And as Gregory and his flock made their way back to Kunwald, they were joined by more and more resolute men and women eager to share in the amazing resilient fellowship.

Early in 1464 the Brethren gathered in a Synod at Reichenau. The terrible fragility of their community's existence weighed heavily upon them. The torments they had already suffered and the threat of terrors still to be laid upon them; the looseness of their organization; and the uncertainty of maintaining a continuing ministry of upright men through adherent priests, brought them to a tremendous question: should they establish a ministry of their own? Nothing was done in haste; the Brethren treasured the unity of the spirit and they were loath to support any further division in Christendom. Was there nowhere, they asked, a Church with a priesthood 'chosen of God' with whom the Unity might join? Deputies were sent to inquire concerning the standing of the Nestorian Church in India, the Abyssinian Church, the Armenian and the Greek Church in Russia. But nowhere could such a priesthood as the Brethren desired be found.

Another Synod was summoned in 1465, and according to the precedent of Acts 1.25-26 the guidance of God was sought in the use of the lot. The lot had two questions to answer:

Is it God's will that we should separate entirely from the power of the Papacy and hence from its priesthood?
Is it God's will that we shall institute, according to the model of the primitive Church, a ministerial order of our own?

The lot replied 'Yes' to both questions.

At the first Synod of Lhota in 1467, three Brethren—Matthias of Kunwald, a farmer; Thomas of Prelouic, a clerk; and Elias of Chrenouic, a miller—were chosen by the lot to be the first priests of the Unitas Fratrum. Then the Brethren agreed by a majority that episcopal ordination should be sought. The episcopal office, it was thought, would not only link the Unitas Fratrum more closely to the primitive Church and to the continuing witness of the Spirit in the Christendom of the fifteenth century, but it would also unite the Brethren's congregations more closely among themselves and more readily obtain them 'sanction with the religious public'; their priesthood would have to be acknowledged by the rulers of the realm; and their enemies would find it more difficult to discredit their ministry.

Michael Bradacius was sent to discuss the matter with Stephen, a bishop of the Waldenses in South Moravia. Stephen consecrated Michael as a bishop;[1] and at the second Synod of Lhota in 1467,

---

[1] Stephen did this, said Michael in his report to the Brethren, by the granting of the Lord 'with confidence, and strengthened us thereby, spoke good things, praised the Lord God, and said that the Lord God had done it for the good of our salvation'. See Edmund de Schweinitz, *The History of the Church known as the Unitas Fratrum or the Unity of the Brethren* (Bethlehem, Pa., 1885), pp. 141 f.; Peter Brock, *The Political and Social Doctrine of the Unity of the Czech Brethren in the 15th and early 16th Centuries* (The Hague, 1957).

Bishop Michael re-ordained Matthias, Thomas and Elias, as priests of the Unitas Fratrum. Matthias was chosen by the lot to be the bishop of the Unity and Michael consecrated him. Thus the Brethren took the road which led them into the assured pages of history. The Unitas Fratrum had become the first independent Protestant Church with a ministry of her own. Her episcopal orders have proved valid and unbroken through all the glories and torments of her history to this day.[1]

Persecution upon persecution was heaped upon the Brethren as the events of 1467 became known. 'All the Hussites for denying the absolute obedience to the Pope were hated', wrote the compilers of the *History of the Bohemian Persecutions* (1632), 'but the Brethren for quite casting him off were utterly detested.' But still the Unitas Fratrum continued to grow. By 1500 there were more than 300 churches of the Unity, and as many schools, and at least 100,000 members in Bohemia alone. Wealthy barons, like William von Pernstein, were eager to build churches and houses of prayer for the Brethren on their estates. But, as always, their denominational growth did not blind the Brethren to the ecumenical vision and venture. In an age when true religion was betrayed by bigotry, pomp and bloodshed, the Unitas Fratrum loved and kept tolerance, simplicity and peace. Theology was not despised but little value was set on the learned complexities by which scholars sought to explain the mysteries of the Christian faith. Weight was thrown on those points of doctrine which united the followers of Christ and not on those which would encourage separation. Simply and completely the Brethren agreed among themselves to be 'satisfied with God's Word'. With childlike trust, for example, they took the Lord's Supper and affirmed that 'all who receive the sacrament in truth

[1] It was not until the Second Diet of Spires in 1529 that the Lutheran Reformation used the word 'protestant' and solemnly affirmed the convictions of Protestantism that there can be another kind of Churchmanship than that which was possible under the Papacy and that the Word of God is the standard of Christian faith and practice. The Unitas Fratrum had already confirmed these convictions in theory and practice by 1467, and had already taken her place on the highroad of history along which the other Protestant Churches followed.

through faith, believe and confess that it is the true body and blood of Christ, according to His word and mind, without adding anything, or taking away anything, and rejecting all human explanation'.

The Brethren held fast to the doctrine of the Invisible Church. The Church was a community 'gathered out of the world' by Christ. At the Synod of Reichenau in 1464 they prayed: 'Unite all the children of God in one spirit'. As early as 1474, with what Knox has called 'a fine instinct of adventure', deputies were sent throughout Christendom, to Greece, to Russia, Palestine, Egypt, Constantinople and Thrace, searching for 'godly men, and a truly Apostolical Church to which they might join themselves, and not live solitary and alone'.[1] At a Synod in 1486 the theme of Christian unity was deeply examined. One resolution declared that 'Wherever in any part of Christendom, the Catholic or only saving faith is found in truth, as declared in God's Holy Word—there is the Holy Catholic Church.'

It was acknowledged that should any other body of Christians be found who 'excel us in the knowledge of the fundamental articles of the Christian religion, we ought to submit ourselves to them, and learn of them. If they do not excel us, we are not, on that account, to despise or revile them'. The irenic and ecumenical purpose was unanimously ratified in a Synodal resolution of 1489: 'That if it should please God in any country to raise up sincere teachers and reformers in the Church, we should make common cause with them.'[2] In 1491 a mission was sent to the East in search of kindred spirits. It was led by Luke of Prague, the great Bishop of the Unity, who edited in 1501 the first hymn-book known in the history of Christendom.[3]

The Reformation and Comenius

When Luther's trumpet-blast of Reformation resounded through Europe, the Brethren were quick to hear it. In 1520 they visited

[1] Knox, *op. cit.*, p. 394.
[2] John Holmes, *History of the Protestant Church of the United Brethren* (London, 1825), vol. i, p. 64.
[3] A copy of this hymn-book survives in the Bohemian Museum at Prague, where it was first printed.

Erasmus in Antwerp; in 1522 they went to Luther at Wittenberg; in 1532 Luther printed (and wrote a Preface) to the Brethren's *Confession of Faith*, and in his lectures he told the students that 'there have not arose since the times of the Apostles, any men, whose churches come nearer to the Apostolical doctrine and rites, than the Bohemian Brethren'. In 1540 the Unitas Fratrum extended her acquaintance with the Reformers of Strasburg, with Martin Bucer, Fabricius Capito and John Calvin. There was nothing niggardly about their praise for the Brethren. Bucer wrote, 'Your churches have received a great gift from God: the bond of unity and love, of good order and fellowship'. Calvin shared a deep admiration for their 'good morals, order and discipline'.[1]

The truth is that Luther and the other Reformers were surprised and delighted to find a Church already organized, grounded in the Word of God only, and maintaining a vigorous existence apart from the Church of Rome. And already, too, the innate function of the Unitas Fratrum as a bridge-church was apparent. In matters of faith, the Brethren were closer to Luther; in matters of order, close to Calvin; and they still maintained a window to Catholicism. The Brethren never regarded themselves as a sect. They had not cut themselves off from the Church Universal, but only from its corruptions. In 1534 they declared that they 'had gathered themselves into a Unity for the purpose of using in holy fellowship those good things of the old Church which they in no wise rejected, and those formerly mixed of evil and good which they purged, having rejected only all those doctrines which they knew to be evil'.[2]

The Brethren were intensely aware of the unity of the Reformation; and again, in the strange irony of history, it was by a persecution, intended to destroy them, that they were led to widen and deepen their ecumenical witness. In May 1548, King Ferdinand issued an Edict of Banishment against the Brethren and they made their way into Poland. Under the leadership of George Israel,

[1] For the Brethren and the Reformers see de Schweinitz, *op. cit.*, pp. 230 f.
[2] *A History of the Ecumenical Movement*, ed. R. Rouse and S. C. Neill (London, 1954), p. 89.

Congregations of the Unity were established in Poland, and at length in 1570 they were able to inaugurate the first significant bond of union among the Protestant traditions. By the Consensus of Sendomir (April 1570) the Unitas Fratrum, the Lutherans and the Calvinists, while maintaining their own doctrinal emphases, agreed to recognize the fraternal union and the common faith which existed among them. On Sunday, 28 May, the members of the three communions worshipped in turn in one another's churches as a symbol of their Protestant unity. It is plain to see that the hand and spirit of the Brethren was written large across the Consensus. 'We will end', it declared, 'and bury in perpetual silence all those controversies, strifes and differences by which the progress of the Gospel has been hindered. We rather pledge ourselves to promote peace and public tranquillity, to show love one to another, and with united hearts, agreeably to our fraternal union, to strive to build up the Church.'

During the second half of the sixteenth century, despite the machinations of the Jesuits, the Unitas Fratrum rose to the height of her stature and influence. By their writings and translations—their Kralitz Bible is still a standard of the Czech tongue and literature—and by their music and hymnody, the Brethren became the very hearth of national culture; and by their labours in formulating the *Confessio Bohemica* (1575) with the Utraquists, the Lutherans and the Calvinists, they constituted the rallying point of Protestant unity in Bohemia. And it was by the leadership of their own Baron Wenzel von Budowa that the Brethren stood in the forefront of the struggle for national liberty. Consequently they shared in the general Protestant ruin which followed upon the disaster of the Battle of the White Hill, 8 November 1620. The foremost leaders of the Unitas Fratrum were executed; the Church's lands and property were confiscated; their precious books were burnt; and as a result of the Renewed Ordinance, issued against the Brethren in 1627, the Unity ceased to exist as an organized Church in Bohemia and Moravia. Once more the brethren and sisters took hold of the 'wandering-staff', and in 1628 they set off through the mountains for Poland.

As the exiles reached the boundary between Bohemia and Silesia, high on the reaches of the mountains, they turned and looked back over their native land. A young priest, named John Amos Comenius, prayed fervently for them. He prayed that the light of the Scriptures might not go out for ever in Bohemia and Moravia; and that God would preserve a seed of righteousness which should grow up, however dark the days might be, and restore the Unity once more. And this 'Hidden Seed' was to flower in due time. A Hidden Seed, the fathers of the Neissers and their fellows, remained in their native land and waited faithfully for the great awakening.

It is certain that the memory and character of the Brethren can never perish from the earth while the name of Comenius lives on. 'Comenius', said Sir Ernest Barker, 'is the finest expression, but he is an extension as well as an expression, of the native and original genius of the Brethren.'[1] Exiled for life from his homeland, Comenius became a citizen of the world and a teacher of nations. He revealed to the world the interest of the Unitas Fratrum in education, in toleration, in the ideals of ecumenism and international peace and unity. He knew that the bulwarks of lasting peace must rest on the united witness of the Christian Churches, and he gave himself unstintingly to the ecumenical cause. From the *Labyrinth of the World* to the *Unum Necessarium* in 1667, he sought 'to reconcile Christians (if it should please God) who in various ways to their own hurt and near ruin wrangle concerning the faith'. In *An Exhortation of the Churches of Bohemia to the Church of England*, dedicated to Charles II in 1660, Comenius makes a plea for the 'togetherness' of Christendom: 'O, you Christian people, dispersed throughout Europe, Asia, Africa, America, and the Islands of the Sea, into so many Religions, Sects, Opinions and multiplied into different Ceremonies, what else I pray are you now become, but as those bones of Israel in Ezekiel, scattered abroad in the field of the world! O, that it would please God to bring on that day . . . to command that there be a noise and a shaking, that so the bones may draw one to another, and come together.'

[1] *The Teacher of Nations*, ed. J. Needham (Cambridge, 1942), p. 83.

Amidst all his international activities and the international fame which they showered upon him, Comenius never forgot for one moment that above all he was a bishop of the Unitas Fratrum. He shepherded his scattered flock in their exile; kept alive the traditions of their Church; maintained an underground traffic in books and succour for the Hidden Seed in Bohemia and Moravia; and preserved the orders of the Church for the great day of renewal. In 1660 he published a full account of the genius and organization of the Unitas Fratrum. It was called *De Bono Unitatis*, and contained a Dedication and Exhortation to the Church of England, a concise history of the Unity, the *Ratio Disciplinae*, and copious explanatory notes. With an exquisite tenderness he commits to the Church of England, 'our dear mother, the Church herself'. 'Even in her death', he tells the Anglicans, 'you ought to love her, because in her life she has gone before you, for more than two centuries, with examples of faith and patience.' That the valid ministry of the Brethren might continue he arranged for the consecration of two new bishops of the Church at the Synod of Milenczyn, 5 November 1662. Nicholas Gertich was consecrated and appointed to the Polish province; and so powerful was the belief that the Bohemian-Moravian province of the Unity would arise once more that Comenius's son-in-law, Peter Jablonski, was consecrated and appointed to that province. On 10 March 1699, Peter's son, Daniel Ernst Jablonski, was consecrated a bishop and it was he who handed on the episcopal office to David Nitschmann, the first bishop of the Renewed Unitas Fratrum or Moravian Church, on 13 March 1735.

The Foundation of Herrnhut

This, then, was the historic Church to which the 'Hidden Seed' belonged: the Church which, in the words of Dr Martin Schmidt, had 'exhibited an irenic spirit throughout its history' and striven 'consistently after unity in the essentials of Christianity';[1] the Church which, in the statement of the General Synod of the Unitas Fratrum in 1957, had always 'pointed towards the unity of

[1] *A History of the Ecumenical Movement*, p. 89.

the scattered children of God that they may become one in their Lord'.[1]

Christian David did not forget the Neissers' request for a place of refuge. In 1722, his old friend John Andrew Rothe, minister-elect of the church at Berthelsdorf, introduced him to Zinzendorf. The Count and the carpenter met in the house of the master of the horse. They discussed the oppressive situation of the Hidden Seed in Moravia; and Zinzendorf's response was immediate. 'Let as many as will of your friends come hither,' he said. 'I will give them land to build on, and Christ will give them the rest.' Zinzendorf has told us that it was because of his vow in the Order of the Grain of Mustard Seed that he made this response.[2]

It was on Whit Monday, 25 May 1722, that Christian David burst into the house of the Neissers with the good news from Berthelsdorf. At ten o'clock on the following Wednesday, the first of the emigrants set off through the night. There were ten of them, and all but one were descendants of George Jaeschke: the two brothers, Augustine and Jacob Neisser, their wives and four children—one little boy of six years, a little girl of three and twins of three months; together with Michael Jaeschke and Martha Neisser. They could only take the bare necessities with them; and few could be told for fear of betrayal. Christian David marched at their head. The Jesuits soon set a price on his head, and his lodgings were burned to the ground. Zinzendorf was away in Dresden when the refugees arrived; but on 8 June Christian David and the Neissers were kindly received by the Baroness Gersdorf at the castle. She gave them a cow to provide milk for the children; and she granted them permission to cut as much wood from the forest as they required to build a house—not in Berthelsdorf itself, but in some spot by themselves, not far from the village. A site was chosen on the declivity of the Hutberg (Watch Hill) near the high road from Lobau to Zittau. It was then a dreary wilderness. No wonder the wife of Augustine Neisser quoted Scripture: 'Whence shall we get

---

[1] *Church Order of the Unitas Fratrum (Moravian Church)* (Bethlehem, Pa., 1958), p. viii.

[2] J. R. Weinlick, *Count Zinzendorf* (Nashville, Tenn., 1956), p. 37.

bread in this wilderness?' She was simply told: 'If you believe, you will see the glory of God.'

On 17 June 1722 Christian David felled the first tree for the building of the first house. 'Yea', he cried from the psalm as he wielded the axe, 'the sparrow hath found a house, and the swallow a nest for herself.' Already—so undaunted was his faith—he envisaged the area divided into quarters and the direction of the streets marked out. By 7 October the house was ready. At the end of December, Zinzendorf was bringing his bride, the Countess Erdmuth Dorothea Reuss, home to Berthelsdorf. As he drove through the wood he saw the light in the new dwelling; going into the house, he cordially welcomed the Moravian refugees and knelt down with them to thank God and to commit them to the Saviour's keeping.

Already the name of the exiles' colony had been pronounced. It was Heitz, Zinzendorf's steward, who first gave it the name of Herrnhut (The Watch of the Lord). 'May God grant', he had written to the Count in July 1722, 'that your Excellency may be able to build on the hill called the Hutberg a town which may not only itself abide under the Lord's Watch (Herrnhut), but all the inhabitants of which may also continue on the Lord's Watch, so that no silence may be there by day or night.' And already the words of prophecy had been spoken over the little colony: in his sermon at the installation of Rothe as minister of Berthelsdorf, Pastor Schafer had declared with great emphasis: 'God will place a light on these hills which will illumine the whole land; of this I am assured by living faith'.

3

THE WATCH OF THE LORD

Disputes at Herrnhut

BETWEEN 1722 and 1727 Zinzendorf's ecumenical ideals and practice endured their first baptism of fire. They emerged glowing and big with promise. Despite every difficulty, the young count was determined to make Herrnhut an embryo united Christendom, an example to the world of co-operation between Christians of different confessions and churches. And he succeeded. Bishop Daniel Ernst Jablonski, in a letter to Zinzendorf, was lost in admiration at what 'your Excellency has found and brought to pass in Herrnhut: namely, that the Evangelical Brethren do dwell there in Unity; and there is only One Shepherd and One Fold there.'[1]

As Herrnhut grew, so did the variety of its inhabitants. Refugees came from Moravia and Bohemia and from different parts of Germany, all eager to worship in freedom and to uphold those principles which Catholic persecution had failed to purge out of them. Besides the descendants of the ancient Unitas Fratrum, there came exiles from Lutheran homes, Pietists, Reformed, Separatist, Anabaptist, Gichtelian and Roman Catholic—and their variety brought the almost inevitable discord. Indeed, the continued existence of Herrnhut hung by a very slender thread.

There was external opposition and increasing internal dissension. Zinzendorf was accused by the neighbouring authorities of harbouring a nest of heresy and of enticing the tenants away from their landlords. Nothing could have been further from the truth. On arrival at Herrnhut, the emigrants were subjected to the

[1] *Acta Fratrum*, p. 8.

strictest examination, and only those who could prove that they had come purely for the gospel's sake were allowed to stay. Internal discord grew because it was not to be expected that men and women who had left everything for conscience' sake would lightly surrender their own individual and peculiar convictions. There was open rebellion when Pastor Rothe demanded from his pulpit in Berthelsdorf that all the refugees should acknowledge the Lutheran Confession and enter the Lutheran fold. There was further disagreement concerning the nature of the wafer to be used at the Holy Communion; concerning the open or the individual confession to be made before the Communion; and concerning the liturgical form of the church services. Christians of so varied a character and origin naturally enough had their rough corners, and an ecumenical diplomat of the most patient perseverance and understanding was required.

Great as were his services to the Moravian Church and her witness in later years, Zinzendorf's whole attitude and action was never more decisive and reconciling than during this early period of disruption. He was the Squire of Berthelsdorf and, as he wrote, 'I could easily have found means to rid myself of many of these people who gave me so much trouble'; but he believed that the Lord had a great work for him to do among them. He felt that full liberty of conscience in all points was most agreeable to the will of God. He was tolerant; he was patient; he was forbearing. He had a wonderful gift and freedom in conversing with individuals on intimate matters pertaining to the soul. He was still in State service at Dresden, but in all the periods he could spare from that city he held the whole stage in Herrnhut: he gave it depth and quality and character. He strove constantly for the unity of the Christianities. He spent the autumn of 1724 there and during that time he requested all the refugees to call upon him in private at his house and discuss with him the points at issue. Three whole days and nights were given to conversations with the Brethren: they remained in session without thought of food; they separated at two o'clock in the morning and assembled again three hours later. Zinzendorf impressed upon them that sects have 'a certain connection with knowledge but not with love of mankind'. 'He opened to us the Scriptures and gave us direction to understand them aright', commented Christian David; and, he continued, 'this was the first great change and unification of the Brethren'.

But the discord was not healed. It was to grow worse. In February 1725 a distinctive feature, based on an old custom of the ancient Unitas Fratrum, began to take shape in Herrnhut. 'Helpers were appointed', wrote Zinzendorf, 'from among the loyal souls of the Congregation, for exhortation, for observance of the work, for service and almsgiving, for visiting the sick, and particularly for the guidance of souls.' Rank nor wealth nor learning nor age were especial recommendations for such offices: it was spiritual stature alone that mattered. Frederick von Watteville was appointed to watch over the souls of the men; his young bride was set over the women; Mordelt, a tailor, and Gottfried Hahn, a gardener, both of Berthelsdorf, were made a 'teacher' and an 'overseer'; George Jaeschke with Jacob Neisser and his wife, Anna, were appointed 'exhorters'; Augustine Neisser became an 'almoner'; and Christian David with Anna-Lena, a girl cowherd, and Gottlob, a lame young man, accepted the office of 'nurse' to comfort the sick.

But many of the refugees could not brook the discipline of the spirit and the brotherly admonition to which the system of Helpers gave rise. Zinzendorf was busy in Dresden, and Rothe had little gift for the administering of discipline. Emigrants from Moravia still flowed into Herrnhut, but they were often coldly greeted by the inhabitants. Further, the Imperial Government was angered by these emigrations. The property of the emigrants was confiscated; if they were caught they were imprisoned; and those who helped them to escape to Herrnhut were punished with the utmost severity. In the summer of 1726, Zinzendorf learned that David Nitschmann (the Martyr) had been seized while on a journey to his father in Moravia and imprisoned at Kremsir. The Count set off immediately for Kremsir, but all his conversations with Cardinal Schrattenbach, the prince-bishop of Olmutz, on behalf of Nitschmann and the emigrants in general were in vain. It was rumoured that Zinzendorf himself barely escaped the Catholic dungeons.

And now the severest crisis broke out in Herrnhut. During Zinzendorf's absence in Kremsir, a wild and malicious fanatic, named John Sigmund Kruger, came to Herrnhut. Kruger had a pronounced air of sanctity about him; he had a plausible tongue; he had been dismissed from his post at Ebersdorf because of theological differences between himself and Schubert, the court-preacher; and now he had come to a community divided within itself and ready to believe anything proclaimed by a new and determined leader. Kruger denounced the Lutheran Church and urged the refugees to separate themselves entirely from Berthelsdorf. They did so, almost to a man. Christian David followed Kruger. The carpenter built himself a small cottage beyond the boundary of Herrnhut: 'Of what use is it to us,' he asked, 'if the souls are to be entangled in the trammels of a common Lutheranism?'[1] Zinzendorf was denounced as 'the Beast', and Rothe as 'the false Prophet'. To add to the confusion a fanatical sect of Schwenk-felders arrived at the end of 1726. It seemed that every wind of doctrine and division blew through Herrnhut. Rothe thundered in his pulpit; Zinzendorf was still patient and forbearing; but any unity in the Settlement was a thing of rags and tatters; 'in Herrnhut it looks as if the Devil will turn everything upside down', wrote Pastor Schafer on 4 January 1727.

But a new day was beginning to break. Kruger became quite mad and left Herrnhut on 15 January 1727. Zinzendorf was grievously disturbed and almost heart-broken by the dissensions, but he still refused to use his powers as the feudal landlord and he waited patiently for the will of God to reveal itself. In February he wrote a hymn of complete trust:

> Faith breaks through the steel and stone
> And can seize upon the Almighty:
> If one has only faith,
> He can do all!

In March he sent from Dresden a declaration of the errors which had crept into the teaching at Herrnhut. In particular he denounced

[1] *The Memorial Days of the Renewed Church of The Brethren* (London, 1895), p. 87.

the suspicions which Kruger had cast upon the true manhood of Christ. 'Whosoever denies the man Jesus Christ as the Word that was made flesh, and dwelt among us, and who now governs as man all things, denies the Son,'[1] wrote Zinzendorf. In April he came to live in Berthelsdorf so that he might give all his time to the healing of the discords and to caring for the souls whom the Lord had led to his estate. On the first Sunday after Easter, he gathered all the people together at Herrnhut and informed them that, while Rothe would remain in full charge at Berthelsdorf, he himself would be responsible for the Settlement as the assistant pastor and catechist.

The Golden Summer of 1727

Day after day, Zinzendorf went from Berthelsdorf to Herrnhut and spent himself in private and public discussions with the exiles. He devoted himself entirely to their service and to the promotion of their spiritual and temporal welfare. His spirit of love and impartiality, his unbreakable patience and unceasing prayer, began to accomplish his ministry of reconciliation. The first new shoots of fellowship appeared, and there was a general willingness to return to the services in the parish church at Berthelsdorf.

The Moravian Brethren, however, had no desire to be completely absorbed in the Lutheran Church. Zinzendorf had as yet no clear conception of the historic role which the ancient Unitas Fratrum had played as a distinct branch of the Christian Church, and he aimed only at forming the Brethren into an *ecclesiola* within the Lutheran Church; but they insisted more and more on retaining the ancient constitution and regulations of their Church. This insistence had grown more fervent since the arrival of 'the Five Moravian Churchmen' in Herrnhut on 12 May 1724. These brethren—David Nitschmann (the carpenter), David Nitschmann (the weaver), David Nitschmann (the Martyr), John Toeltschig and Melchior Zeisberger—all came from Zauchtenthal in Moravia. Escaping from the Catholic tyranny they had intended to find refuge at Lissa in Poland, but calling in at Herrnhut to see their

---

[1] *Ibid.*, p. 88.

old friend Christian David, they were convinced that here indeed the Lord and his people held watch together and that here their ancient Church might be restored. 'When the Count spoke with the Brethren in this point', wrote Spangenberg, 'they gave him to understand in round and hard words, that they neither could nor would yield in this matter! It was clear that such a constitution was wanting everywhere, and Luther himself had acknowledged to the Brethren that they had the advantage in this respect. If one had doubts about granting them this in the Evangelical Church, and especially if in Herrnhut objections were made against allowing them their own congregation rules and regulations, they would rather take up their staff and wander further.'[1]

Zinzendorf was by no means unsympathetic to the wishes of the Brethren. 'It was only fair', he said, 'that the people who had committed to me their best treasure should not be defrauded of it without their knowledge, or deprived of it with their knowledge.'[2] But the conception of an *ecclesiola in Ecclesia* governed his outlook, and even if he had wished to renew the Unitas Fratrum pure and simple at this time, the Church and State law in Saxony would not have permitted him to do so. He consulted Rothe and the leading Brethren and a compromise was agreed upon. Within a month, a system of rules was drawn up regulating in the first place the legal life of Herrnhut as a civic community; and in the second place its life as a spiritual community. It was to be an *ecclesiola* within the parish church at Berthelsdorf, but with the special recognition of the apostolic discipline and fellowship of the ancient Unity.

And now the golden summer of 1727 began to rise into its full glory: a summer never to be forgotten in the history of the Moravian Church. On the evening of 11 May one of those gatherings— soon to become so characteristic of the Moravian communities— was held: a long and varied *Singstunde* or singing-meeting. On the afternoon of 12 May, Zinzendorf summoned all the inhabitants of Herrnhut to the 'little hall'. He addressed them for three hours. He spoke of the evils of separation and the blessedness of Christian unity. He introduced and explained the *Manorial Injunctions and*

[1] *Zinzendorf*, p. 80.   [2] *Ibid.*, pp. 81 f.

Prohibitions which were to regulate the life of Herrnhut as a civic community and to which the people must adhere by law. And then he laid before the meeting forty-two Statutes called *The Brotherly Agreement of the Brethren from Bohemia and Moravia and Others, Binding Them to Walk According to the Apostolic Rule.* There was no legal compulsion about the Statutes. They were the basis for a voluntary agreement to abide together in Christian fellowship. When all the people came up to Zinzendorf and clasped his hand in token of their acceptance and obedience to the *Injunctions* and the Statutes, the sun blazed out in the heavens. They all took each other by the hand, confessed their sorrow for past dissensions, and bound themselves to live together in mutual love and simplicity.

The ecumenical principle shone out clearly in the second Statute:

Herrnhut shall stand in unceasing love with all children of God in all Churches, criticize none, take part in no quarrel against those differing in opinion, except to preserve for itself the evangelical purity, simplicity and grace.

Zinzendorf and the Brethren were never weary of looking back to the Memorial Day of 12 May 1727.[1] On that day it was decided whether Herrnhut should prove a nest of sects or a living Congregation of Christ; 'and it is not to be expressed in words', the Count wrote, 'how much our Saviour continued to do for that Congregation till the commencement of the winter in the same year. The whole place represented truly a visible tabernacle of God among men, and till the 13th of August there was nothing to be seen and heard but joy and gladness; then this uncommon joy subsided, and a calmer sabbatic period continued.'

In the evening of 12 May it was agreed to elect twelve elders to watch over the faithful observance of the Statutes. Again spiritual stature alone was to be an elder's qualification. Men of high rank and learning were excluded from the office so that it might be filled only by persons of the common class in whom all could rest

---

[1] See *The Memorial Days of the Renewed Church of the Brethren*, p. 42 ff.

their trust and confidence. Christian David—once more united with the Brethren—was elected an elder; and with him there were Augustine and Jacob Neisser; George Nitschmann, a seventy-year-old joiner from Zauchtenthal; Melchior Nitschmann, a twenty-five-year-old weaver from Kunwald; Christopher Hoffman, David Nitschmann, the carpenter, Andrew Beyer and Hans Nitschmann, David Quitt, Frederick Kuhnel and David Nitschmann, the cobbler. After a long conversation, four of these Brethren were elected by the Lot, at 4 a.m. on 20 May, to be 'chief elders': Christian David, George Nitschmann, Christopher Hoffman and Melchior Nitschmann. The simple fellowship of the whole venture is caught by Zinzendorf's description of young Melchior Nitschmann standing at the back of the room 'in shirt sleeves and braces' as his election was announced.

The Count was chosen as the Warden with Frederick von Watteville as his assistant, and together with the elders they watched over every detail of the temporal and spiritual life of the Settlement.

By night as well as by day Herrnhut was to become a visible tabernacle of God. On 21 May all the male inhabitants from the age of sixteen to sixty, without any regard for rank, were assigned to take their turn in announcing the 'night watches'. On 6 July, Zinzendorf wrote a hymn with which the watchmen were to greet the sleeping or the waking community in the slow hours:

> The hour is come: through darkness steals the day;
>   Shines in your hearts the morning star's first ray?
> The clock is two! who comes to meet the day,
>   And to the Lord of days his homage pay?
> The clock is five! while five away were sent,
>   Five other virgins to the marriage went!
> The clock is six, and from the watch I'm free,
>   And everyone may his own watchman be!

Under Zinzendorf's untiring inspiration, every opportunity was seized for mutual edification and fellowship. Statute No 12 had referred to 'the conversion of souls' as a chief object in Herrnhut, and it was openly said that when the people awoke in the morning, the first thing they heard was who had been converted the night before. The Spirit was not quenched: no matter his training or his standing, anyone who felt moved to do so was quite free to speak to his fellows—and they would listen gladly. Zinzendorf tells of the 'ministry' of Martin Dober, the master potter: 'At five o'clock he held a meeting. To it came learned and distinguished people. At nine o'clock a visiting count, nobleman or professor, found him barefoot in his workshop. That was acceptable to them. They sat down before the potter's wheel and listened to the voice of the priest.' 'That', Zinzendorf concludes, 'was the divinity in old Herrnhut.'

Firmly believing it to be the will of God, Zinzendorf had thus begun to mould a divided band of refugees of different denominations into a united and witnessing Congregation: but all through the summer, the people seemed to be waiting and preparing for a still more signal visitation and commandment from the Lord. In June, Zinzendorf and his family took up their new residence in the Herrschaftshaus at Herrnhut, before the walls of their apartments were dry. Sunday 2 July was a day of great blessing: the Count preached in Herrnhut; Pastor Schwedler preached in Berthelsdorf; and Rothe preached in the grave-yard. All three places were thronged with hearers. The whole neighbourhood was ablaze with thanksgiving to God. On 4 July the Statutes were confirmed again with the signatures of the people of Herrnhut. On 19 July and the following week the practical genius of Zinzendorf for the expression and quickening of Christian fellowship gave birth to the 'Bands' without which, he said, 'the Brethren's Church would never have become what it was'. A Band consisted of two or three or more persons of some spiritual kinship who met together privately and conversed concerning the state of their hearts, and exhorted, reproved and prayed for one another. Zinzendorf divided the whole number of the brethren and sisters into these Bands and appointed one person at the head of each group. It is important to remember that in these Bands, as in all the organizations at Herrnhut, there was nothing artificial or forced; the members of one Band often changed to another, so that gradually they became acquainted and heartily united with the whole community. If at any time no advantage appeared from these Bands, they were given up for a time and after a while renewed with a visible blessing. It is also pertinent to remark that 'cells of prayer', after which modern Christendom is reaching in order to renew and deepen its spiritual life and unity, were commonplace in the Herrnhut economy and in the Settlements which, guided by Zinzendorf, the Moravians were to organize around the world.

By day and night Zinzendorf continued to give himself to his work as the unordained catechist in Herrnhut. It was meat and drink to him; his house was never shut; and he visited the entire membership, helping, praying and guiding those in need. On 16 July he prayed with great efficacy amongst the young people. Besides the obligatory night-watch, small groups of the single Brethren held night-long vigils of prayer and meditation which proved a real repose in God and in which Zinzendorf himself often joined. On 22 July ten of the Brethren, including Christian David, Melchior Nitschmann and Leonard Dober, covenanted together to meet frequently on the Hutberg in the God's Acre to pour out their hearts in prayer and singing and mutual exhortation.

From 22 July to 4 August, Zinzendorf was absent on a visit to Baron Gersdorf in Silesia. It was on this journey that he discovered the historic character of the Unitas Fratrum. In the Zittau Library he chanced upon the *Ratio Disciplinae* of Comenius and from the Preface he learned of Kunwald and Lhota and Sendomir and the early ecumenical vision of this ancient and irenic Church. He drew up an extract in German from the *Ratio* and on his return he gave it to the 'Hidden Seed' in Herrnhut. Immediately they recognized the similarity between the *Statutes* and the ancient Discipline. 'We discovered therein', wrote one Moravian, 'the finger of God, and found ourselves, as it were, baptised under the cloud of our fathers, with their spirit. For that *spirit* came again upon us, and great signs and wonders were wrought among the Brethren in those days, and great grace prevailed among us, and in the whole country.'

There was indeed a great grace prevailing in Herrnhut. When Christian David suggested that in the public discourses a study should be made of the Epistles of John, 'there was evidence of the fire of love', records the Settlement *Diary*. There was a contagious and a holy expectancy. It would seem as if the people of Herrnhut were being led inevitably, step by step, to the Pentecost of 13 August—the very crown of that golden summer and the original of all the wonders in Christian service and the glorious witness to Christian unity which were to follow. On 5 August Zinzendorf and fourteen of the Brethren spent the whole night in religious conversation and prayer. At midnight a large company assembled in the Hutberg for a prayer-meeting; they greeted the dawn with the verse—'He is the Sun of Righteousness which rises with resplendent grace'. Whilst conducting the afternoon service at Herrnhut on 10 August, Rothe was so overcome by the nearness of God that he sank down into the dust before him. The whole congregation followed the pattern of the pastor and they continued together until midnight, praising God and covenanting with one another, with many tears and earnest supplications, to dwell together in love and unity. In the morning Rothe delivered an invitation to Zinzendorf and all the people of Herrnhut to attend the celebration of the Lord's Supper at Berthelsdorf on the following Wednesday, 13 August.

Since this was to be the first Communion of the reconciled community, Zinzendorf visited every house in the Settlement and, in a friendly and familiar manner, prepared the families for the coming celebration. He also prepared forty-six questions for two young girls, Catharine Heintschel and Anna Friedler, who were to be confirmed. All the brethren and sisters gathered together in the evening of 12 August and all were deeply moved as the two young girls answered the questions and confessed the Lord Jesus Christ as their Saviour. Catharine and Anna spent the rest of the night in prayer and meditation.

The great day of 13 August dawned: the great day which was to manifest the Lord's blessing on the faith of the 'Hidden Seed' and on Zinzendorf's prodigious zeal and industry in his vineyard; the day which has always been regarded as the spiritual birthday of the Renewed Unitas Fratrum or Moravian Church.

Early in the morning, Rothe gave an address at Herrnhut on the meaning of the Lord's Supper. Then as the people walked the mile to the church at Berthelsdorf, little groups of two or three were seen to converse closely together in mutual friendship and love. The experience of the preceding weeks, it was said, had humbled the exiles under the conviction of their individual sinfulness, need and helplessness, and taught them to think meanly of themselves and kindly of one another. All seemed to be awaiting an extraordinary visitation at the church. The service opened with the hymn 'Deliver me, O God, from all my bonds and fetters' and then Rothe pronounced a truly apostolic blessing and confirmed Anna and Catharine. The whole congregation responded with a fervent *Amen*. They all knelt down and sang:

> My soul before Thee prostrate lies,
> To Thee, its source, my spirit flies.

And this was accompanied with such a powerful emotion that loud weeping almost drowned the singing. Several brethren prayed with great power and fervour. They prayed not only for themselves, but for their brethren still living under persecution; they prayed for those who taking the name of Christian were yet separated from one another; and in particular they prayed that Christian David and Melchior Nitschmann, absent on a visit to Sorau, might be led at the same hour 'into true heart's fellowship' with them. Zinzendorf made a penitential confession in the name of the congregation, and Pastor John Suss of Hennersdorf pronounced the absolution. An inner anointing flowed through every person and with inexpressible joy and love they all partook of one bread and one cup and were 'baptised into one spirit'. All were convinced that, partaking of the benefits of the Passion of the Lamb in real fellowship with one another, the Holy Spirit had come upon them in all his plenitude of grace. They had already been one *body* in a religious community with its own Statutes, but now from this day they were one *spirit*. The Herrnhut *Diary* describes how 'those who formerly could not forbear, fell on one another's neck in the graveyard before the church and pledged themselves together most sincerely; and so the whole congregation came back to Herrnhut as newborn children'.

The Consequences of 13 August

Just as the Unitas Fratrum had been born at Kunwald in the bonds of Christian fellowship, so at Berthelsdorf this ancient Church was renewed in the same constraining unity with Christ and his Christians. Let a Moravian of that time describe the scene once more. 'On the 13th day of August 1727,' wrote Arvid Gradin, 'all the members of this flock in general were touched in a singular manner by the efficacy of the Word of reconciliation through the Blood of Christ, and were so convinced and affected that their hearts were set on fire with new faith and love towards the Saviour, and likewise with burning love towards one another; which moved them so far that of their own accord they embraced one another in tears, and grew together into an holy union among themselves, so rasing again as it were out of its ashes, that ancient Unity of the Moravian Brethren.'[1] Of 13 August, Christian David wrote: 'It is truly a miracle of God that out of so many kinds and sects as Catholics, Lutheran, Reformed, Separatist, Gichtelian and the like, we could have been melted together into one.' 'From that time on', said David Nitschmann, 'Herrnhut became a living Congregation of Christ.' 'Then were we baptized by the Holy Spirit Himself to one love,' said Spangenberg. 13 August, Zinzendorf concluded, 'was a day of the outpouring of the Holy Spirit upon the Congregation'; it was 'its Pentecost'.[2]

So rich was the experience of fellowship and assured unity 'through the Blood of Christ' that it inevitably expressed itself in terms of organization and action. And Zinzendorf was quick to perceive this, to guide and strengthen the irresistible tide of that

[1] *A Short History of the Bohemian-Moravian Protestant Church of the United Brethren.* In a letter to the Archbishop of Uppsala, Primate of Sweden (London, 1743), p. 34.
[2] See *Memorial Days*, pp. 103 ff.

fellowship, the *koinonia* with the Lamb, with each other and with all who gathered at his Cross. On the very same day of 13 August, when the worshippers arrived back in Herrnhut—about noon—from Berthelsdorf, seven little groups continued to talk over the great blessing they had received. 'In order for them to be able to stay undisturbed together', wrote Spangenberg, 'our Count sent to each of them something from the kitchen for lunch which they ate together in love.'[1] And thus with food and drink and brotherly conversation and the singing of hymns, the first spontaneous revival of the primitive Christian *Agape* or Lovefeast was made. The Congregation and Choir Lovefeasts have remained in the Moravian Church since that time as the distinctive expression of that fellowship which each member has with his brethren and sisters in Christ.

On 27 August, twenty-four brethren and twenty-four sisters covenanted together to spend one hour each, day and night, in praying to God for his blessing on the Congregation and its witness. Encouraged by Zinzendorf, this covenant spread wider, and for over a hundred years the members of the Moravian Church all shared in the 'Hourly Intercession'. At home and abroad, on land and sea, this prayer-watch ascended unceasingly to the Lord. Thus all the Moravian ventures for the Lamb and for unity in him were begun and surrounded and ended in prayer. Only thus can great things for God be attempted.

But the experience of 13 August did more than to quicken the organization of the fellowship at Herrnhut: it sealed and clarified that ecumenical vision which Zinzendorf and the 'Hidden Seed' shared in common. More than ever it was realized that true Christian fellowship cannot survive within the small walls of any one congregation or denomination: it must always look beyond itself and reach out to the wider and yet ever wider circles. We have seen how the ancient Unitas Fratrum searched for kindred souls across the continent of Europe and beyond. It was now the glory of the Renewed Unitas Fratrum (or Moravian Church), after the overwhelming experience of fellowship in the summer of 1727, to

[1] See *Memorial Days*, pp. 103 ff.

act upon the simple truth that to be a Christian is to be involved in a mission to the whole world. Unity and mission are inseparable. Herrnhut was to become the clearing-house for Christian news and ventures in many lands. As the news of its growth and character reached the outside world, visitors flocked to the 'Watch of the Lord', and as many as fifty letters a day were received asking for more information and requesting the pleasure of a deputation.

The golden summer had reached its consummation. The evangelical truth that a genuine fellowship, grounded in the gospel of Christ Crucified, must inevitably express and multiply itself in a valiant witness and service was gloriously vindicated. To quote but one snatch of evidence, the people of Herrnhut became 'the vital leaven of European Protestantism'.[1] At one with each other in the fellowship of the 'Blood and Wounds of Jesus', the former exiles now set themselves to bring all the world into that same unity with him. Within five years they had organized the bonds of their own unity in Herrnhut; they had sent out itinerant messengers to awaken the 'sleeping' in the other churches and to provide them with a common place of encounter and co-operation in the *Diaspora* societies; they had plans in the making for the mutual discovery, enrichment and service of all the denominations; and the first two missionaries had been sent out to begin the realization of the 'daring dream of carrying the Christian Gospel throughout the world'.[2] It is not too much to say that here in the ecumenical workshop of Herrnhut the pattern of the modern Christian witness and expansion was being shaped.

The people of Herrnhut sought nothing for themselves; they sought only to be used by the Lamb of God as a leaven of his unity wherever he might call them. They sang:

> Herrnhut shall exist no longer,
> Than the works of Thy own hand
> Uncontrolled rule in its borders:
> And be love its sacred band;

[1] Knox, *op. cit.*, p. 390.
[2] K. S. Latourette, *History of the Expansion of Christianity* (London, 1939), vol. ii, p. 66.

> Till ripe for Thee, and found worthy
> As a good salt to be scattered,
> That the Earth thereby be bettered.[1]

And it was Zinzendorf who, with a burning vision, a passionate conviction, an incomparable eloquence, an amazing range of inventiveness and thoroughness of application, and a magnificent torrential energy, directed and developed this ecumenical worship and witness. He was an educative force of the first magnitude, and he spent the rest of his life and all he possessed in moulding a grand army of the Lamb.

---

[1] *A Collection of the Hymns of the Children of God in all Ages from the beginning till now.* In two parts, designed chiefly for the use of the Congregations in union with the Brethren's Church (London, 1754), pt. ii, p. 254.

4

THE ADORATION OF THE LAMB

No Christianity Without Fellowship

'EVERYTHING in Herrnhut is extraordinary,' wrote Henry Rimius in 1753.[1] He was attempting to discredit Zinzendorf and the Moravians with ludicrous praise. But even some of Zinzendorf's friends have praised him for purposes which he never entertained. Herrnhut and the other Settlements which the Count inspired in Europe and America were not experiments in socialism or communism or Utopian idealism. Their extraordinary character lay in the fact that they were one of the most remarkable experiments in the realm of Christian service that Christendom has ever seen. The total life of the community—men, women and children—was organized for the adoration of the Lamb and the advancement of his Kingdom on a world-wide scale. The whole social and economic existence of the inhabitants was precisely framed to embody and carry forward that clear religious and ecumenical purpose. Herrnhut certainly provides a profound subject of interest to the sociologist, but for Zinzendorf such an interest would have been simply beside the point.

The adoration of the Lamb was the constant theme in Herrnhut by day and by night:

> Lamb of God
> Thanks and praise to Thee are due;
> O accept our adoration
> For the blessings ever new

[1] *A Candid Narrative of the Rise and Progress of the Herrnhuters* (London, 1753), p. 20.

Flowing from Thy life and passion:
May our hearts and lips with one accord
Hail Thee Lord![1]

'It is impossible', wrote a Moravian minister of the mid-eighteenth century, 'to utter any divine truth, or to speak anything, which one might call complete without mentioning the LAMB, our Saviour. This must be the anointing, and the salt, the principal ingredient of every matter, of every sigh, of every writing, of every sermon, yea of every thought.'[2] And indeed, turn where you will to any record of Herrnhut during these years—diary (of which the Moravians were so fond), history, manifesto, sermon, litany or hymn—the name of the Lamb, his praise, the benefits of his passion and our unity in him, run through them all.

'Our meetings', said Zinzendorf, 'should be conducted with reverence and solemnity. Whether we teach or pray, whether we sing or meditate, whether we remain sitting or standing, or in what situation soever we may be . . . we should conduct ourselves as in the presence of the Lamb with a feeling of reverence and adoration.'[3] There were at least three meetings for the whole Congregation each day of the week. The day began at four o'clock in the summer and at five in the winter with singing in the hall. At eight o'clock in the morning and evening all the people met to pray and to praise the Lamb and to read and hear the Scriptures. There were special services for the children and for the aged and infirm. The day ended as it began with singing.

The Sundays were veritable feasts of worship: from five in the morning till gone nine at night the voice of praise could be heard. Following the 'morning blessing', the Choirs held their own particular services from six o'clock until nine; the children's meeting was at ten, and the morning worship in the Berthelsdorf

---

[1] A verse of a hymn by the Countess Zinzendorf (*Moravian Hymn Book*, 1912, No 272).

[2] Francis Okely, *Dawnings of the Everlasting Gospel-Light* (Northampton, 1775), p. 12.

[3] A. Bost, *History of the Bohemian and Moravian Brethren* (London, 1834), p. 381.

church was at eleven; at three, the visitors (who flocked to see Herrnhut) and those who had been unable to attend the morning service met together to hear the Berthelsdorf sermon repeated by Zinzendorf or some other brother; at four, there was another service in the parish church, and at eight another at Herrnhut; and at nine o'clock the young men hallowed the ending of the Sabbath with the singing of hymns as they marched round the boundaries of the Settlement.

On different Saturdays of the month there was a celebration of the Lord's Supper, a solemn Day of Prayer for the children, a conference of the chief officials of the Congregation, and a Congregation Day on which news of the itinerant 'messengers' and missionaries at home and abroad was read out by Zinzendorf. There was no narrow parochialism at Herrnhut.

No Christian community has ever done more than Herrnhut to preserve the individual soul in its living adoration and fellowship in the Lamb. There was indeed a special care of souls, and it was the plain and direct character of Zinzendorf's own communion with the Lamb which enabled him to speak so freely and intimately and wisely with everyone in these matters. From ten in the morning until two in the afternoon, before the celebration of the Lord's Supper, Zinzendorf spoke with the communicants concerning their spiritual life and growth. He also planned a method of visitation whereby every member was approached at least every fourteen days. The visitors would converse with the members during walks, or in the house, before or after working hours. Sometimes a visitor would suddenly step into a workshop and, without saying a word, look at his brethren. The look was well understood; it conveyed the inquiry, *Is the Lamb in your thoughts?*

Although Zinzendorf recognized that there could be no substitute for the personal devotion of each single heart to the Lamb, he allowed none of the morbidities or excesses of a too-exclusive preoccupation with the state of one's own soul to arise. Like the ancient Unitas Fratrum, Zinzendorf and his Moravians took most seriously that element of the original Christian faith which looked beyond the salvation of the individual to the redemption of the human race and indeed of the whole created order. This world-view of course was grounded in the conception of the fellowship of all men in Christ and it effectively discountenanced any of that exaggerated individualism to which all religious revivals seem to be prone.

As in the congregations of the ancient Unitas Fratrum, fellow-ship—*koinonia*, 'participation', 'having a joint share'—was the very warp and woof of the life and mission of Herrnhut: so much so that Zinzendorf has been said to have added Fellowship as a third Sacrament in the Protestant Church; and as Bishop Shawe has said 'there is truth in this remark—for the Moravian, fellowship is a signal means of grace, as necessary as any Sacrament, and the practical cultivation of fellowship is an outward and visible act accompanied by an inner spiritual meaning.'[1] This fellowship did not arise out of the natural endowments of man; it was a gift of the Lamb and proceeded from him as the unchanging source and pre-server of all true unity among men. Such fellowship, said Zinzen-dorf, breaks down all barriers of creed and constitution, of taste, outlook, class and race because the Lamb is at the centre of it. And it is not so much a fellowship of kindred minds but fundamentally of kindred hearts. The 'heart' is here designated 'as the centre of a man's personality, the innermost core of personality, the point where a man's attitude to his fellow-men is fundamentally decided and from which his practical treatment of his fellow-men is con-trolled.'[2] 'Even amongst people who talked half a dozen or half a score of theological languages', anyone with this gift of fellowship, said Zinzendorf, 'could understand them all'. In one of his finest hymns, Zinzendorf expressed the root and ground of this Christian fellowship which he sought to spread across the world and into all the Churches so tragically divided from one another:

> Christian hearts, in love united,
>   Seek alone in Jesus rest;
> Has he not your love excited?
>   Then let love inspire each breast;

[1] C. H. Shawe, *The Spirit of the Moravian Church* (Bethlehem, Pa., 1957), p. 24.
[2] *Ibid.*, p. 21.

Members—on our Head depending,
Lights—reflecting Him our Sun,
Brethren—His commands attending,
We in Him, our Lord, are one.

Zinzendorf recognized no Christianity where there was no fellowship. To illustrate this point, the story is often told of Zinzendorf's visit to Halle in 1736. A young lieutenant named Charles Henry von Peistel sought an interview with him, and the following conversation took place—

Z: Do you love the Lord Jesus?
P: Yes; but not so ardently as I should wish to love Him.
Z: Whose fault is that? is it the fault of the Lord Jesus, or is it your own?
P: It must be my own.
Z: Do you hold fellowship with any of Christ's people?
P: Here you see two common soldiers who also love the Lord Jesus.
Z: Do you visit one another?
P: Yes; we meet almost every day.
Z: That is fellowship: *I acknowledge no Christianity without fellowship.*[1]

Zinzendorf had an undoubted genius for fellowship, and the extraordinary variety and richness of the organization in the Moravian Settlements which he inspired testify to the reality of that fellowship. The Night-Watch, the Hourly Intercession and the Lovefeasts continued. The Bands prospered and ninety of such groups met in Herrnhut at least twice a week to 'converse heartily and kindly over their whole hearts with one another . . . for more complete nurture in the Lord'. These Bands were effective expressions of both the individual and the corporate responsibility for preserving the fellowship of the 'Lamb's Congregation'; and they were groundsprings of evangelism. They sprang up wherever the Brethren went and their impress was emphatic. In 1733, for example, they spread to Herrnhut's neighbours in Zittau, Gorlitz, Ebersdorf, Jena and Hennersdorf; the professors and students at Tubingen met in their Bands.

---

[1] *The Moravian Magazine* (London, 1854), vol. i, p. 337.

But perhaps the most outstanding expression of the fellowship in the Lamb, in the social and economic life of Herrnhut, was the 'Choir' system. It arose partly from the force of circumstances, and partly from Zinzendorf's vivid insight into the particular demands of each stage in an individual's life and into the quite modern conception of the value of group interests and activities. It formed the basis of the Count's theory of education and it helped to make possible the Moravian mission to the whole world. The Lamb was again at the centre. The Congregation was divided into 'Choirs' or groups according to sex, age and 'condition'—married or single. The Elder or Labourer over each choir would lead its members into a deeper fellowship with one another and the Lamb by the contemplation of some particular incident or period in his life and the gospel story. For the Married Choirs there was Christ, the Bridegroom of his Bride, the Church; for the Single Brethren there was Christ in the wilderness and the itinerant ministry; and for the boys there was Christ in the Temple and the carpenter's shop.

Within each Choir there was a constant and detailed pastoral visitation. Each Choir was subdivided, for the purposes of religious instruction and according to their inward growth, into classes of about ten or twelve persons. Each had its own special services, its own hymns and liturgies, festival days and Lovefeasts; and each had its own Cup of Covenant (Luke 23.17):

> Assembling here, a humble hand,
> Our covenantal pledge we take,
> We pass the cup from hand to hand,
> From heart to heart, for His dear sake.

Ten such Choirs were developed under the guidance of Zinzendorf. Separate Choir Houses were established and for their maintenance it became necessary to establish an 'Economy' or 'Diacony' —an economic organization embracing trades, handicrafts, farming and joint housekeeping. On 29 August 1728, the single Brethren led by Martin Linner, a baker by trade, moved into their Choir House which besides being a home was also a centre of handicraft industries and a place of training for apprentices in the army of the Lamb. On 4 May 1730, the single Sisters, led by the mature and gifted Anna Nitschmann—only fifteen years old—entered into their own house and covenanted together to serve the Lamb wherever he might call them and to remain unmarried if his service required it. On 7 September 1733 the Married Choir came into being and dedicated themselves to the Lamb's service for the sake of the children. Gradually there evolved the choirs of the widowers, widows, the youths, the big girls, the little boys, the little girls and the infants-in-arms. The Sisters wore a distinctive ribbon: blue for the wives, white for the widows, pink for the young women and red for the girls under eighteen. All were ready, or being trained to be ready, to obey the command of the Lamb and to serve him wherever and whenever and at whatever he decided. The children in their choirs and schools and orphanages were the responsibility of the whole community; their parents, perhaps far away on the Mission field, rested in the knowledge that their sons and daughters at Herrnhut were being loved and cared for with that same love in the fellowship of the Lamb as they themselves would have given them. The Labourer over each choir met Zinzendorf each week to lay before him whatsoever hindered or blessed the work of the Lamb in the souls committed to his charge. Thus the army of the Lamb, the 'Saviour's Armoury',[1] was fashioned; disciplined and ready to go forth into all the world—at a moment's notice.

The Lamb Slaughtered and Conquering

Yet the life at Herrnhut was centred not simply in the adoration of the Lamb, but in the adoration of the *slaughtered* Lamb. It was the scandal and the offence of the Cross, with the 'Lamb that was slain, torn and massacred', that Zinzendorf led the brethren and sisters of Herrnhut to shatter the Deistic composure of eighteenth century established Christianity and the varnished decorum of polite society. It was with the 'Lamb and Blood' that deliverance was brought to the poor, and refuge to the outcast, and the

[1] Spangenberg's phrase.

Evangelical Revival set aflame. It was a 'Blood and Wounds' theology that carried the fellowship of all men in Christ to the Negro, the Eskimo, the Indian, the Hottentot, and to the 'separated' Christians in Europe and America.

In a winter Conference which Zinzendorf summoned at Marien-born in 1740, it was declared: ' "The Lamb Slain" was from the beginning, the foundation upon which our Church was built.'[1] We know that the Lamb was a constant symbol of the ancient Unitas Fratrum and that in this symbol they saw their hope and comfort in times of oppression, and the assurance of final victory. But it was in the age of Zinzendorf that the slaughtered Lamb became the very seal and watchword of the Moravians and their mission.[2] It was Edeling, the Count's tutor at Gross-Hennersdorf, who had pointed the way for him. 'He spoke to me', wrote Zinzendorf, 'of Jesus and his wounds.' One day in 1734, when he was burning wastepaper, Zinzendorf found one slip of paper which had escaped the fire. On it was written: 'Oh! let us in Thy nail-prints see our pardon and election free.' He took these words to be a message from God. Only the slaughtered Lamb could reveal the love of God to man and unite all men in his service. And more and more from that day the 'Blood and Wounds' theology—the Scourging, the Thorns, the Nail-prints and the Wounded Side—rang throughout Herrnhut and wherever the Moravians carried the gospel:

> In Jesus' blood their element
> They swim and bathe with full content.

Such a theology was open to grave abuse and there was a time in the 1740s when the Moravian witness was marred by its excesses;[3] but it *was* the message of Redemption and Reconciliation

[1] F. F. Hagen, *op. cit.*, p. 20.
[2] The seal which Bishop Daniel Ernst Jablonski used for the certificate of Zinzendorf's consecration as a Moravian bishop, 20 May 1737, was inscribed with a Lamb carrying a flag on a badge with flowers and with the motto— *Vicit Agnus Noster Eum Sequamur*. This seal of the ancient Polish Unitas Fratrum was taken over by the Moravian Church.
[3] See C. W. Towlson, *Moravian and Methodist*, p. 129, and J. R. Weinlick, *op. cit.*, pp. 198–206.

which God gave to the Moravians to bring to an age that had largely forgotten it, and it arose out of a profound and decisive insight which Zinzendorf had into the mystery of God's way with sinful and separated men. Zinzendorf challenged the fashionable world and the fashionable Churchianity of his day not with neat theological theories but with the slaughtered Lamb of God who was truly Man. Zinzendorf and his preachers held up for all to see the grossness and the ugliness—the spittle dripping from his lips—of the Lamb, smitten for our iniquities, upon the Cross. He showed how all the inherent restrictions and marks of weakness of the human life of Jesus made all the more glorious the wondrous condescending grace of God to men. He showed how every feature of the 'humiliation of Jesus'—the poverty, the toil, the sweat of brow, thirst and homelessness—set forth the reconciling love of God; still more, the sufferings, the temptations, the agony in Gethsemane and the wounds of the Cross. 'We must carry an *Image* of our Incarnate God in our hearts', said Zinzendorf, 'and whoever is too refined and philosophical for this, is an unconverted person and an alien from God's Household.'[1] Before this image of the Lamb, all the pomp of man's possessions and the prejudice of his class and the pride of his intellect and the bigotry of his denominations must fall down; all that separates man from man, and Christian from Christian, must be laid down at the foot of the Cross.

At a Synod in October 1740, under the chairmanship of Zinzendorf, the Moravians made this declaration:

The difference between those zealous servants of God, who, in Germany, by some were called Pietists, in England, Methodists, in France, Jansenists, in Italy and Spain, Quietists, in the Roman Church in general often known by the character of preachers of repentance and ascetics, but in the Protestant Church generally thought Mystics, on the one side, and our Oeconomy on the other, is this: the former strive either for an alteration of the behaviour, or the thoughts, or both; or for an alteration in the religious worship; or are for abolishing all the external Part: We preach nothing but the Crucified Christ for the heart; and we think that when any one

[1] *Maxims*, p. 217.

gets hold of Him, all that is idle vanishes away from such a person, and all necessary good comes, together with the living and abiding impression of the loving and faithful Lamb of God, who was once a mortal Man in reality.[1]

No Christian community has thought more constantly or prepared more thoroughly than Herrnhut for the celebration of the passion of the Lamb. During Passion Week itself, passages were read each day from the Harmony of the Gospels describing the last days of the Lamb on earth: the passages were unaccompanied by any commentary or sermon but were left to make their own direct and unadorned impact upon the soul of every listener. Before the Lord's Supper all the members of each Moravian Settlement throughout the world went to the 'Speaking' at which they were examined concerning their fellowship with the Lamb and given leave to attend the Sacrament—'those who have gone off from their former purity and simplicity of heart, being excluded'. Before the administration of the Sacrament, the New Testament custom of foot-washing was observed. The Elders washed the Brethren's feet, and the Eldresses washed the feet of the Sisters. This custom persisted down to 1818. The abundance of singing was typical, and still is typical, of Moravian worship. The theme throughout was unity in adoration, centred in the Lamb slain for all men. And at the close of the Lord's Supper, a Covenant verse was sung during which the members gave to each other the kiss of peace and the right hand of fellowship:[2]

> We who here together are assembled,
> Joining hearts and hands in one,
> Bind ourselves with love that's undissembled,
> Christ to love and serve alone:

[1] *Acta Fratrum*, p. 83.

[2] 'This "right hand of fellowship" is a unique feature in the history of Christian rites. Undoubtedly the Communion is regarded in other Churches too as a "corporate act" symbolised by the sharing of bread and wine in fellowship; but one would think that this would signify for most people the fellowship of the worshipper with his Lord. The fellowship with one's brethren and sisters is given a special and visible symbol only in the Moravian Church, so far as I know.' C. H. Shawe, *op. cit.*, p. 24.

O may our imperfect songs and praises
Be well-pleasing unto Thee, Lord Jesus:
Say, 'My peace I leave with you';
Amen, Amen, be it so.[1]

Unlike the Pietists who demanded in every conversion the sorrows and 'conflict of repentance', Zinzendorf and the Moravians found nothing for moaning or pity at the Cross, but only the source of an intense and overwhelming gratitude which made them

ever ready
Cheerfully to testify
How our spirit, soul and body
Do in God our Saviour joy.[2]

At the Cross they found a full assurance of faith which admits of no doubt or fear; a repose in the blood of Christ; a firm confidence in God, and a persuasion of his favour; serenity and tranquillity of mind; with deliverance from all outward and inward sin, not by frontal assault or the rigours of a planned asceticism but by abandoning themselves entirely to the leading of the Lamb. They lived ' in Christ'. The Pietists were God's grammarians: they looked at their own sins first and then at the Cross and found an abundance of tears. Zinzendorf taught the Moravians to be God's troubadours: they first looked at the Cross and rejoiced because they found there a covering for all their sins. Zinzendorf once declared: 'We are the Saviour's happy people.'

Without an awareness of their supreme happiness in the Lamb we cannot hope to understand the willingness of Zinzendorf and his brethren and sisters of Herrnhut to sacrifice themselves and all that they possessed to carry the power and the fellowship of the Crucified Christ across the world. It was this sheer happiness which set them singing at all times, and never has a band of Christians sung so much, at their work and in their worship, as these Moravians. It singularly opposed the 'spleen' and melancholy of the eighteenth century. This happiness of the Moravians, amidst the perils of the sea, first made John Wesley intimately acquainted with

[1] *Moravian Hymn Book*, No 675.   [2] *Moravian Hymn Book*, No 646.

his own lack of a saving faith.[1] It was this happiness which made the Moravians an envied people.

Their unquenchable happiness utterly freed them from any fear of death. They would put on no clothes of mourning for the soul 'returning to one's native land'; at a funeral they sang hymns of triumph, and the four trombones sounded out from the cupola of the Hall. The Moravians have been called the 'Easter People' and perhaps no other body of Christians has so compellingly expressed their adoration of the risen Lamb. The beautiful Easter Liturgy of 1749, largely from Zinzendorf's hand, is one of the most impressive of all liturgies and reveals a noble and intimate adoration of the Lamb who has conquered.[2] It was while the Single Brethren were at prayer on the Saturday evening before Easter, 1732, that they agreed to gather together in the God's Acre, on the Hutberg, before sunrise the next morning. At four o'clock on that Easter Sunday they began to sing their *Alleluias* around the graves and waited for the Easter sun to rise. As it appeared the Elder or the minister shouted for all to hear: 'The Lord is risen!' The people gave back the glad response: 'He is risen indeed!' And then the hymns and the trombones re-echoed in the stillness of the early dawn and the Congregation rejoiced in the everlasting truth of the resurrection of the Lamb once slain. And still, wherever in the world Moravians meet, the early Easter morning service is observed.[3]

The Work of Herrnhut

The inhabitants of Herrnhut kept themselves near to the heart of the Lamb for one all-consuming purpose: to serve him wherever he might call them. For no other purpose was Herrnhut organized. The English word *service* does not convey the exactitude of the meaning involved. Bishop Shawe prefers the German word

[1] John Wesley's *Journal*, vol. i, p. 142.
[2] See *The Moravian Hymn Book*; Philip Schaff, *Creeds of the Evangelical Protestant Churches* (London 1877), p. 799; W. A. Curtis, *History of Creeds and Confessions of Faith* (Edinburgh, 1911), p. 136.
[3] See A. L. Fries, *Distinctive Customs and Practices of the Moravian Church* (Bethlehem, Pa., 1949).

Dienersinn. 'It means to feel oneself to be a servant, to have the mind or attitude of a servant; it describes a living character rather than a quality, a type of person whose mind is dominated by the will to serve.'[1] It did not matter in what labour or office that service was to be given. The dustman in the street, the night watchman on his rounds, the carpenter at his bench felt himself 'called' to the service of the Lamb as much as the preacher or the missionary on some foreign soil. Each in his own way belonged to the apostolate of the Lamb and was a soldier in his army. The tailor who went to work at his trade and support the missionary Schumann in Surinam was as truly in the 'service' of the Lamb as the missionary himself.[2]

As each member saw his own particular work as service to the Lamb there was no room for idleness in Herrnhut. Often sixteen hours of the day were given to work. 'In a Church we must work,' said Zinzendorf; 'we should not work to live, but live to work.' All idle thoughts and idle pleasures were discouraged; all superstitions, stories of ghosts and quackery of any kind were banned; all popular entertainers and entertainments, such as play-acting and dancing, were forbidden; all extravagance of dress was frowned upon; parasols and fans were never seen. The sisters wore their distinctive ribbon on their white straw hats, and the brethren dressed simply in grey or brown. But this was no mere negative Puritanism. There simply was no time to think about worldly amusements and adornments; and there was no money to spare.

The discipline was strict and it was administered without fear or favour by Zinzendorf and the twelve Elders. The Choir Labourers met regularly with the Elders to discuss their particular members; the Helpers on Tuesdays; the Teachers on Wednesdays; the Overseers on Thursdays; the Monitors on Fridays. The whole life of

[1] Dr D. T. Niles has a comment which gets near to the heart of the matter: 'It is damnably easy to serve . . . but it is not so easy to be a servant.' *The Preacher's Calling to be Servant* (London, 1958), p. 52.

[2] 'It cannot occur to a brother working in the stable or in the professional callings that he is not working for the Saviour; whoever is faithful in lesser, temporal things is just as honourable a servant of Christ as a preacher or missionary' (Moravian Conference minute). 'The farmyard becomes a temple of grace, full of priestly activity' (Spangenberg).

Herrnhut was in the purview of Zinzendorf and the Elders—the rates and taxes, the upkeep of buildings, the cleaning of the streets, the care of the poor and sick, the education of the children, the arrangement of marriages, the reprimand and final expulsion of the thief and the drunkard, as well as the despatch and encouragement of the missionaries. And the discipline was most positive in purpose: it was a discipline of co-operation for the common good so that the health of the whole fellowship in body and soul might be preserved for the service of the Lamb.

There was no general community of goods at Herrnhut but every member sat very loosely to the things of this world. The Single Brethren and the Single Sisters, in particular, shared most things in their own Choir Houses and were ready at an instant to go forth in the Lamb's service. No man in Herrnhut worked for himself alone. All worked to ensure that none need be in want and that the 'warriors' might be trained and equipped. 'It is very important', Zinzendorf declared, 'that the Brethren should labour everywhere in the true spirit of the community, not seeking their own advantage, but that of the whole Church. To consult our own ease at the very time that we are sending hundreds of brethren into all parts of the world, in the midst of poverty and distress, and while the Church altogether is so poor, would be an affront to the Cross of Jesus. I am therefore of the opinion that we ought to reject every man who shows a disposition to seek his own ease and advantage, and if he be a brother, we ought not to trouble ourselves with his complaints.'[1]

The conditions of trade and business were strictly regulated. Inspectors were appointed to see that each person was employed to the best advantage, that the work was well done and sold or paid for at a reasonable price. No competition in trade was permitted; no business could be started without consultation, and none that were deemed unnecessary were allowed; and if a thing could be purchased in Herrnhut, no one could go elsewhere to buy it. All

---

[1] Bost, *op. cit.*, p. 377. Cf. John Wesley: 'The Count's house—a small, plain building like the rest; having a large garden behind it, well laid out, not for show, but for the use of the community.' *Journal*, vol. ii, p. 19.

differences in business had to be settled within a week. A board of arbitrators was set up to advise or settle in these matters, and if any brother went to law he was expelled from the community.

The Lamb blessed the sweat of the brow and faithfulness in business at Herrnhut where 'even a child of four will be able, by plucking wool, to serve the Gospel'. The wool-spinning of the Single Brethren prospered; the weaving and delicate embroidery of the Single Sisters came to be renowned in the courts of Europe; the firm of Durninger achieved an international reputation; the Congregation's farm and bakery became models for the whole area, and all the profits were put into a common fund—the Treasury of the Lamb.

No wonder Bishop Jablonski exclaimed: 'When I read the intelligence from Herrnhut, it is as if I saw the mode of life of the primitive Christians reproduced, and exhibited to the view of the Christian world.' And when John Wesley visited the Settlement in 1738 he was constrained to write in his *Journal*: 'I would gladly have spent my life here. . . . Oh when shall THIS Christianity cover the earth, as the "waters cover the sea"?'[1]

Herrnhut was a haven of peace, with its two hundred houses, built on a rising ground with evergreen woods on two sides, gardens and cornfields on the others, and high hills at a short distance. It was a haven of faith in a world of infidelity; of unity in a world of division. But still more. When Wesley visited Herrnhut the Moravians had already proved themselves more than an example. Zinzendorf had transformed a band of refugees of differing Christian traditions into a united missionary army—and history supplies no similar example:

> Own Thy Congregation
>   O Thou slaughtered Lamb;
> We are here assembled
>   In Thy holy name.[2]

[1] Vol. ii, p. 28. [2] *Moravian Hymn Book*, No 685.

5

THE ARCHITECT OF MISSIONS

The Birth of the Missionary Movement

THE Pentecostal experience of 13 August 1727 renewed and illumined the missionary ardours which Zinzendorf had felt as a young student. And now the Count and his Moravians prepared to act upon the simple ecumenical truth that to be a Christian is to be involved in a mission to the whole world: a truth largely lost in Zinzendorf's own day, and by no means honoured in our own.[1] At the very first of the monthly Congregation 'Prayer Days' at Herrnhut, 10 February 1728, the Count introduced plans for evangelism in the West Indies, Greenland, Turkey and Lapland. To those who doubted the possibility of those ventures, he replied: 'The Lord can and will give grace and strength for this.' The very next day twenty-six of the Single Brethren, under Leonard Dober, made a covenant together to pray for the world-mission of the Church and to go forth instantly at the first clear call.

In April 1731 Zinzendorf attended the coronation of Christian VI in Copenhagen and there he talked with Anthony Ulrich, a negro slave from the island of St Thomas in the West Indies. Anthony told Zinzendorf how often he had sat on the shore of the

---

[1] The Divinity Faculty of Wittenberg denounced missionary advocates as false prophets. In 1722 the hymnologist Neumeister of Hamburg closed his Ascensiontide sermon by giving out the hymn:

> 'Go out into the world', the Lord of old did say;
> But now: 'Where God has placed thee,
> *There* he would have thee stay!'

A. L. Drummond, *German Protestantism since Luther*, p. 62.

island and sighed his soul towards Christian Europe; and how his brother Abraham, and his sister, Anna, and many other of the slaves in the West Indies longed to hear the Gospel. At last the Count saw his missionary dreams coming to life. On 23 July he told Anthony's story in Herrnhut; that same night Leonard Dober, the potter, and Tobias Leupold heard a voice in their dreams calling them to St Thomas island. As these two brethren walked together in the brushwood on 24 July they revealed their dreams with a holy amazement to each other and knelt down to pray for guidance. Within half an hour, as they marched with the other Single Brethren past Zinzendorf's house, they heard him say to Pastor Schafer at the doorstep: 'Sir, among these young men are missionaries to St Thomas, Greenland, Lapland and other countries.' On 25 July, Dober and Leupold wrote a letter to Zinzendorf and made the first recorded offer of service in Moravian Missions.

But, as was their custom, the Moravians did nothing in haste. On 29 July Anthony told his story in Herrnhut and warned his hearers that no one could hope to bring the gospel to the slaves without first becoming a slave himself. Despite the eagerness of Dober and Leupold, nearly a whole year went by and no decisive action was taken. On 16 June 1732 Dober wrote again to Zinzendorf: 'If another brother will go with me', he pleaded, 'I am ready to become a slave myself.' That same day the Lot decided that Leupold must stay in Herrnhut; but as for Dober, the answer was: 'Let the lad go, for the Lord is with him.' David Nitschmann, a carpenter and a married man, was chosen to go with Dober to St Thomas and return to report after four months.

On 18 August the whole Congregation gathered in Herrnhut and in a meeting of rare fervour and expectancy they sang a hundred hymns to cheer the missionaries on their way. At three o'clock in the morning of 21 August 1732, Dober and Nitschmann stepped into the carriage outside Zinzendorf's house. The Count drove them the fifteen miles to Bautzen. There they knelt by the roadside. Zinzendorf drove back to Herrnhut; the other two brethren set out on foot for Copenhagen, bundles on their backs, thirty shillings in their pockets, and the invincible all-embracing love of

Christ in their hearts. Thus the modern world-wide missionary movement was born.[1]

'By 1760', said Dr Gustav Warneck, the eminent historian of Protestant Missions, 'the Moravian Church had done more for the heathen than all the other Protestant Churches put together.'[2] By 1740, sixty-eight Moravian missionaries had been sent out; and by the time of Zinzendorf's death in 1760, no less than 226 missionaries had gone to destinations ranging from the Arctic to the tropics, from the Far East to the American mid-west. Something of the rich variety of the world-mission directed by Zinzendorf can be gathered from the dedication of the *Text Book* which he compiled annually for his Moravians wherever they might be:

The Good Word of the Lord 1739 from all Prophets for His Congregations and Servants at Herrnhut, Herrnhaag, Herrendyk, Pilgerruh, Ebersdorf, Jena, Amsterdam, Rotterdam, London, Oxford, Berlin, Greenland, St. Croix, St. Thomas, St. Jan, Berbice, Palestine, Surinam, Savannah in Georgia, among the negroes in Carolina, among the savages in Irene, in Pennsylvania, among the Hottentots, in Guinea, in Litvonia, and Esthonia, Lithuania, Russia, along the White Sea, Lapland, in Norway, in Switzerland, Isle of Man, Shetland, in Prison, on the journey to Ceylon, Ethiopia, Persia, on Visitation to the Messengers among the Heathen, and otherwise on Land and Sea.[3]

And as the venture grew so did it become more international in character: Moravians from Germany, Holland, Great Britain and America proclaimed the Gospel to the Negroes, Hottentots, Eskimos and American Indians. This 'daring dream of carrying the

---

[1] The Moravian 'pride of place' in this movement is confirmed by Dr Norman Goodall, *A History of the London Missionary Society* (London, 1954), p. 1. It should be noted that the earlier Anglican societies, SPCK and SPG, directed their activities, not to the natives (as the Moravians did) but to 'the King's loving subjects' beyond the seas, and they 'confined themselves to particular fields'.

[2] J. E. Hutton, *A History of Moravian Missions* (London, 1922), p. 186.

[3] See W. N. Schwarze, 'History of the Text Book of the Moravian Church', *Transactions of the Moravian Historical Society* (Bethlehem, Pa., 1944), vol. xiii, pt. 3–4, p. 145.

Christian Gospel throughout the world'[1] became an epic of self-less devotion and unbreakable courage and at its very heart beat the pulse of Zinzendorf's ecumenical vision—all men of every land are one in Christ the Redeemer. Under Zinzendorf's leadership these Moravians accepted, lived out and traced out this vision across the world in their own blood. 'If you go to Labrador', the missionary Drachart was told, 'the Eskimos will kill you.' 'If they kill me', he answered, 'they will kill me.'

In All the Continents

Arvid Gradin wrote in 1743 that the Moravian missionaries suffered a thousand hardships; but nothing daunted them—imprisonment, persecution, shipwreck, plague, privation, death—'all these things', Gradin continued, 'only increased the zeal and fervour of our Brethren, whose firm resolution it was, rather to die, than to go away without Fruit.'[2] The preaching to the slaves of St Thomas was a slow and toiling business; little scope was given by the State; no public meetings were permitted and Dober and Nitschmann patiently visited the Negroes one by one as the sun went down; even where the planters did not openly oppose the missionaries, they hindered the work by the poverty of their own Christian witness. On 17 April 1733 Nitschmann returned to Herrnhut as previously arranged. On 11 June 1734, Dober's old friend, Tobias Leupold, arrived in St Thomas with a company of fourteen brethren and four sisters. They had come to evangelize in the neighbouring island of St Croix and to tell Dober to return to Herrnhut where he had been elected the Chief Elder. With him sailed away to Europe the first fruit of his mission: Carmel Oly, an orphan boy.

Death walked with these missionaries almost every step of the way. Their voyages across the world in their small and over-crowded ships were perilous undertakings. Leupold's company had taken seven months to reach St Thomas; and there the malaria,

---

[1] K. S. Latourette, *History of the Expansion of Christianity*, vol. iii, p. 66.
[2] *Op. cit.*, p. 57.

the dysentery and polluted water threatened them. Before they crossed over to St Croix, three of their number had died of the yellow fever. The first service in the island was the funeral of a little child. By January 1735, ten more of the company, including Leupold himself, had died; in the May, eleven more brethren arrived from Herrnhut not knowing what they would find—no news of the earlier mission had reached Europe. By July, seven more were claimed by the fever; nine more, miserably weakened by the fever, were forced to sail home—and three of these were lost on the voyage. In all there had been twenty-two deaths in two years. No wonder Moravian historians have christened this episode, the Great Dying. But it was by no means unique in the missionary story: more than thirty of the brethren perished in the early years of the venture in Surinam. The faithful warriors 'went home to the Lamb with exceeding joy', and their ranks were eagerly filled by fresh volunteers from the Saviour's Armoury.

On 30 September 1736 three converts were baptized—Peter, Andrew and Nathaniel. Around them the first Mission Congregation on the island of St Thomas was formed. For the first time the Negro boys and girls were taught to read and write when, in accordance with the Moravian educational approach, the missionary Frederick Martin started a small school in his house. Martin's colleague, named Freundlich, married Rebecca, a mulatress. But the planters led by Pastor Born of the Dutch Reformed Church determined to stamp out the Moravian mission. No trick was too mean for their purpose. They summoned the missionaries to give evidence in a case of theft, and when they refused for conscience' sake to take the oath, and further refused to pay the fine for not taking it, they were imprisoned in the Castle. But each evening the slaves came to hear Martin and Freundlich preaching through the bars of their cell, and joined in the singing which kept the planters awake.

In January 1739 Zinzendorf himself arrived in the island, intent to see the progress of the mission at first hand. The Count was not a good sailor, but he dealt with that difficulty in his usual direct and simple way. 'Since I had so much to do', he wrote later, 'I talked with the Saviour, saying that it would not be convenient for me to be sick, and so I became well even before we sailed.'[1] He was greatly angered by the treatment of the missionaries. 'I burst into the Castle like thunder', he wrote home to the Countess. Not only did the Governor apologize to Zinzendorf personally and release the prisoners, but he also promised them security from persecution and guaranteed them freedom to preach and worship as they pleased. Eight hundred Negroes were now responding to the Gospel. 'St Thomas is a greater marvel than Herrnhut,' the Count declared. In three crowded weeks he preached daily in the open air and organized the island into four districts with Martin as the Superintendent. On his way home in March 1739 Zinzendorf secured from the Danish king an edict of complete religious liberty for the Moravians in the Danish West Indies, together with protection from their enemies.

The pattern of the mission story began to take shape: first, a period of opposition and often bitter persecution from the white planters; and then a gradual and fitful encouragement, followed by open-hearted co-operation. Some of the West Indian planters invited the Moravians to preach to their slaves. Some of the Governors even granted the missionaries free postage for all their communications to Europe. And as the years went by the Moravians carried the Gospel to the rest of the islands in the Caribbean crescent.

Meanwhile the reconciling Gospel had been preached in the Arctic. Zinzendorf had also met two Eskimo boys at Copenhagen in 1731; he presented the need and the challenge to the Congregation at Herrnhut; and on 20 May 1733 the good ship *Caritas* landed three Moravian missionaries at Godhaab in Greenland. The difficulties were immense. The language was a thick barrier; the Eskimos were hostile; they came to the missionaries only to beg

[1] It was on this voyage that Zinzendorf gave his memorable description of the Moravians. As the ship entered the harbour of Tappus in the island of St Thomas, he spoke his thoughts aloud: 'Suppose the Brethren are no longer here; what shall we do in that case?' Immediately George Weber, one of the Moravian missionaries, replied: 'In that case, we are here.' '*Gens aeterna, diese Mahren* (an Imperishable Race, these Moravians),' the Count exclaimed.

or to steal; they had no ear for the Gospel. 'The sooner you fools go home, the better,' they told the Moravians. The cold and darkness were intense. Scurvy was rife. The provisions ran so low that the missionaries nearly starved; they lived on shell-fish and raw sea-weed, and they came to regard a little oatmeal mixed with train-oil as a delicacy. In 1734 a virulent fever and epidemic of smallpox ravaged the West Coast. Oblivious of their own danger the missionaries nursed the sick and received little thanks for their pains. And still no converts were made. But on 6 March 1735, Matthew Stach, Frederick Bohnsich and John Beck signed the Covenant of the Three Brethren, in which they vowed never to leave their posts. 'We will never forget', they agreed, 'that we came hither resting upon Christ our Saviour, in whom all the nations of the earth shall be blessed, not on the principle of sight but of faith.'[1]

As long as the story of Moravian Missions is told, the evening of 2 June 1738 will never be forgotten. As John Beck sat in his tent translating the Gospels into the native tongue, a group of Eskimos gathered round him. They asked him about his work, and he began, as he had often tried before, to open up the questions of dogmatic theology with them. But they turned away. And then in an inspired moment, John Beck slowly read the verses he had just translated from St Matthew's account of the Agony in Gethsemane. 'And He took with him Peter and the two sons of Zebedee, and began to be sorrowful and very heavy. And He fell on His face and prayed, saying, Father, if it be possible, let this cup pass from Me.' Where argument had failed, the story of the Suffering Saviour prevailed—a lesson the Moravian missionaries never forgot. A young Eskimo, named Kayarnak, demanded with eager amazement: 'What is that? Tell me that again; for I, too, would be saved.' All that night the passion of the Lamb was told. On Easter Sunday 1739, Kayarnak, the first Eskimo Christian, was given the name of Samuel and baptized with his wife, Anna, his son, Matthew, and his daughter, Aima. In 1747 five Eskimos accompanied Matthew Stach to Herrnhut, to Zeist and to London where they were received by George II and the Royal Family.

[1] Hutton, *op. cit.*, p. 68.

It is certain that as these Moravian missionaries tackled their task of preaching to the heathen natives in the corners of the globe they were looked upon as fools or madmen by many so-called Christians. When George Schmidt arrived in Cape Town on 9 July 1737 he overheard a conversation in the tavern where he proposed to lodge. 'I hear', said one Dutch farmer, 'that a parson has come here to convert the Hottentots.' 'What! a parson?', another laughed, 'Why the poor fool must have lost his head!' 'And what sir, do you think?' a waiter asked the stranger sitting quietly in the corner. 'I am the very man,' Schmidt replied.

In a quiet valley, one hundred miles east of Cape Town, known as Bavianskloof (Glen of Baboons), George Schmidt established the oldest mission station in South Africa. He built a house and planted a famous pear tree; he formed a school and taught the Hottentots how to read and write; he taught them how to till the soil; and he revealed the Lamb of God to them in all these things. On 31 March 1742, in the peaceful Steenbrans river, he baptized one of his pupils named Willem—the first fruit of African missions. And when four more of the Hottentots were converted, he founded the first native Congregation in South Africa. But the old web of persecution, of lies and racial prejudice, spun itself more vigorously. Because Schmidt had baptized the Hottentots, with only a letter of ordination to qualify him for this ministerial office, the Dutch clergy were able to drive him out of the country in March 1744.

In 1739 Spangenberg reported to Zinzendorf from Pennsylvania that 'maybe the hour of grace has sounded' for the Indians. Certainly there was a splendid field of opportunity for the Moravian missionaries. The Red Indians at this time swarmed across the vast lands of North America: there were the Mohicans in Dutchess County, New York; the Shawanese in the Wyoming Valley; the Iroquois in New York, Pennsylvania and the areas bounded by the Lakes Huron, Eerie and Ontario; and the Delawares in north-west Pennsylvania and Ohio. In response to the challenge a young Moravian of twenty-two years arrived in New York on 16 July 1740, prepared to live and preach and die among the Indians. Christian Henry Rauch soon found the opportunity he was seeking.

He met a drunken chief of the Mohicans, named Wassampah, and a Delaware Indian, named Shebosh, who understood the Dutch language. They promised to take the young missionary to their village of Shekomeko, about twenty miles east of Rhinebeck and on the borders of Connecticut. They forgot their promise but Rauch followed them, and in the month of August he began his fearless witness in the Indian village. It was a vice-ridden place, but soon it began to change into a place of the Lamb. Meetings were held daily and at the monthly Prayer-Day an account was given of the Moravian missions in other parts of the world; the Moravians were always ready to strike the note of a world-wide Christian unity! By the end of 1742 there were thirty-one Christian Indians.

Wassampah, the drunken Mohican of Shekomeko, proved to be a most distinguished convert to the Christian faith and the subject of many a sermon, romance and legend.[1] He is known to history as Tschoop, the German phonetic spelling of Job—the name he had received amongst the Dutch traders in New York. Immediately the new life and witness of this redeemed pagan won fresh victories for the Lamb he had learned to love. Indians came from far and wide, not for drinking and dancing now, but to see and hear Tschoop. He preached eloquently and his countenance, likened to that of Luther by Spangenberg, was full of power and peace. It was at a Conference in the Moravian Settlement of Bethlehem in Pennsylvania in 1745 that Tschoop told of his own conversion, of Rauch's preaching and of the constraining simplicity of his faith and courage. Others, said Tschoop, had spoken to him of God and of a morality, but the Moravian missionary

came into my tent, sat down beside me, and spoke nearly as follows: 'I come to you in the name of the Lord of Heaven and Earth. He sends to let you know that He will make you happy and deliver you from the misery in which you lie at the present. To this end He became a man, gave His life a ransom for man, and shed His Blood for him'.

---

[1] Wassampah (or Tschoop) is generally recognized as the original of Chingachgook in *The Last of the Mohicans* by Fenimore Cooper. Tschoop died of smallpox on 27 August 1746 in Bethlehem, Pa., and his grave can still be seen there in the Moravian 'God's Acre'.

When he had finished his discourse he lay down upon the board, fatigued by the journey, and fell down into a sound sleep. 'What kind of man is this?' thought I. 'There he lies and sleeps. I might kill him and throw him out into the wood, and who would regard it? But this gives him no concern'. I could not forget his words. They constantly recurred to my mind. Even when I was asleep, I dreamed of the blood which Christ shed for us. I found this to be something different from what I had ever heard, and I interpreted Christian Henry's words to the other Indians. Thus, through the grace of God, an awakening took place before us. I say, therefore, Brethren, preach Christ our Saviour, His sufferings and death, if you wish your words to gain entrance among the heathen.[1]

Meanwhile the Moravians had entered South America and attempted to spread the gospel among the Negro slaves in Paramaribo, the capital of the Dutch colony of Surinam. But when their efforts had been defeated by the hostility of the planters and the clergy, they struggled south through one hundred miles of swamp and jungle to preach to the Arawack Indians. In 1740 a mission station was set up at Pilgerhut, and there Solomon Schumann laboured amongst the wild and murderous Indians and baptized 400 of them before he died of the fever in 1760.

The first mission to Labrador—'The land God gave Cain'—ended in tragedy. John Christian Ehrhardt, a Moravian pilot and missionary, and three of his friends landed on the south-eastern coast of Labrador in July 1752 and called their house 'The Valley of Hope'. A small company led by Ehrhardt sailed farther north, but only a few sailors returned to the southern base: Ehrhardt, the captain and four sailors had gone ashore and were never heard of again. Yielding to the plea of the mate to help in the navigation of the ship, the other missionaries returned to Europe.

Zinzendorf did not believe that any heathen race as a whole could

[1] For the further development of the Moravian mission to the North American Indians, and for an account of David Zeisberger, the great apostle to the Indians, see K. G. Hamilton, *John Ettwein and the Moravian Church during the Revolutionary Period* (Bethlehem, Pa., 1940) and E. E. and L. R. Gray, *Wilderness Christians* (New York, 1956).

be converted until the Jews had embraced Christianity. But he was convinced that in every nation there were a few selected spirits, 'Candace-souls' (Acts 8.27), who were eager and waiting for the truth. Accordingly, he sent his 'Flying Scouts' across the world in all directions in search of these chosen people. In 1734 Andrew Grassman led a mission to Lapland; in 1736 he attempted with Daniel Schneider and Michael Mieksch to reach the Samoyedes and other tribes of the Arctic, but after imprisonment in Archangel they were sent back to Herrnhut by Catherine II under threat of death by burning if they dared to return. In 1737 Henry Huckoff and Christian Protten, a mulatto, set off for Guinea on the West coast of Africa, but within a few months of arriving there Huckoff died of the fever. Hoping to prepare the way for a series of missions to the East Indies, Mongolia and Persia, David Nitschmann and Dr Eller went to Ceylon in 1739, but again the opposition of the Dutch clergy prevented any progress. Abraham Richter preached to the stricken slaves in Algiers and nursed them until he himself died of the plague in July 1740. In that year too, the Moravian mission in Wallachia came to an end with the death of the friendly Hospodar of Bucharest.

In 1742 Conrad Lange, Zechariah Hirschel and Michael Kund set out to preach the gospel to the Buddhist Calmucks and beyond them to the Chinese. But at St Petersburg they were denounced as spies and thrown into prison for five years. At their trial the judge declared that 'their behaviour and manner would convert the heathen'. Such was their spirit of utter trust in the Lamb that they called their prison a 'Hall of Grace'. On his way to Livonia in 1743 Arvid Gradin was also imprisoned in St Petersburg for three years. In 1747 a doctor and a surgeon, Hocker and Ruffer, attempted a Moravian mission to the descendants of the 'Wise Men from the East'—the Kurds of Persia. Near Bagdad they were robbed and left for dead by the bandits. At Ispahan they were well received but the civil wars crushed any hopes of an immediate mission in Persia. In 1752 Dr Hocker learned Arabic in Cairo and attempted to reach the Copts of Abyssinia. The Coptic Patriarch accepted the letter which Hocker brought from Zinzendorf and called it most pertinently 'a piece of his love to all Christians'. A medical mission in 1756 proved no more successful: Dr Hocker and George Pilder were shipwrecked near Jedda, lost their medicines, and barely escaped with their lives from the Arabs.

Missionary Strategy

Behind this vast stretch of enterprise lay the driving and organizing hand of Zinzendorf. His strategy and sweeping vision, his great heart and 'warrior' songs, kept the pulse of the missions beating. Like most worthy generals, he knew in theory and practice the hazards of the campaign; and he sent his warriors into the battlefield and kept them there, with all the resilience that the most agonizing and perpetual prayer could secure. His was the valour as well as the vision. And the missionaries loved him like a father; they called him 'Papa'; he selected them; he instructed them; and by the arrangement of visitations and an endless correspondence he did all that he could to keep in touch with them and their problems. Often 150 letters lay on his desk awaiting a speedy reply. The task was prodigious, but so was the man.

It was an essential part of the genius of Zinzendorf that whilst he inspired a grand zeal and daring in the Moravian missions he yet saw to it that they were rooted in method. There was a relentless sanity in his direction of the enthusiastic world-mission. If it was difficult to become a member of the Moravian Church in the eighteenth century, it was still more difficult to become one of her missionaries. Only members of the Church were accepted; they had to volunteer; and Zinzendorf tested them with the shock of the severest discouragement and delay. Even if the missionary was already on board ship, Zinzendorf would order him to disembark if he entertained any doubt at all about his 'call'. It was well that the aspirant missionary should 'count the cost' before he set out, rather than hinder the work later by faint-heartedness and disloyalty. The volunteer was required to reply to a list of questions which Zinzendorf laid before him in the presence of the whole Congregation. For example, when Dr Regnier wished to go out to

Surinam as a medical missionary, the procedure was as follows.

Z: What makes you think you are called to this work?

R: I have long felt an inward call to preach the Gospel to others.

Z: What do you intend to do in Surinam?

R: I will do my best to earn my living and to bring sinners to Christ.

Z: How do you intend to get there?

R: I shall simply trust Christ to shew me the way.

Z: How long do you intend to stay there?

R: I shall stay there either till I die or till the Elders call me to another field.

Z: How do you propose to treat your wife?

R: I will love her with all my heart; but I shall not allow my love for her to interfere with my work.

Z: How will you treat the Congregation you are leaving?

R: I will honour and obey Herrnhut as my spiritual mother.

Z: How will you behave if you have to wait a long time before you go?

R: If I have to wait for a ship, I shall simply regard the delay as the will of the Lord.[1]

Zinzendorf supervised the instruction of the missionary-candidates in medicine, geography and languages.[2] On the truly cosmopolitan *Prayer-Day*, held each month, the Congregation was informed and inspired by the letters and visits from the Brethren already on the mission field. We read that on 24 September 1734, at one of these Lovefeasts of rye bread and water which went on far into the night, there were forty brethren ready to go out to the heathen; on such occasions some of the converts from the mission field could be seen and heard singing to the Lamb in their native tongues. At one service in Herrnhaag, John Cennick heard a hymn sung in twenty-two different languages; and at a Lovefeast held in

---

[1] Hutton, *op. cit.*, p. 171.

[2] Well-meaning friends have overstressed the simple ignorance of these pioneer Moravian missionaries. There is the reply of Zinzendorf to a sarcastic question concerning the meetings presided over by Leonard Dober, the potter: 'When we come to the reading of the Old Testament, the potter is accustomed to use only his Hebrew Bible. If he is ill, or absent, the Count endeavours to fill his place; but when Dober is present, the Church loves best to hear him.'

Bethlehem, Pennsylvania, on 21 August 1745 there were Eskimos, Arawacks and Mohicans present in addition to the European missionaries. Certainly no Protestant Church had ever directed her efforts to so many different races; never had one Protestant Church possessed so varied, so mobile and itinerant a band of missionaries and ministers; and they moved from one field of service to another with often an almost bewildering rapidity. As Bishop Ettwein, the missionary statesman in North America, declared, 'My life becomes a travelogue, purely and simply.'[1]

In a constant flow of conferences, speeches and writings, Zinzendorf made clear to the missionaries the message they were to preach, the policy they were to adopt, and the whole purpose they were to pursue. He produced at least fourteen pamphlets of *Instructions* on mission affairs.[2]

There was no doubt about the message. 'Tell them about the Lamb of God till you can tell them no more', Zinzendorf wrote to George Schmidt away among the Hottentots. The Lamb of God is the only theme of the world-mission: 'the missionary cause is Jesus Christ's affair in His world.' In his *Plan of a Catechism for the Heathen* (1740), Zinzendorf made it clear that only the 'Blood and Wounds' theology could bring a heathen soul to Christ. The heathen knew that a God existed and they needed no immediate lectures in apologetics. They desperately needed to hear of the Saviour who died for them. When he spoke of the Lamb, wrote David Zeisberger, the Moravian apostle to the Indians, then he could 'bring an Indian by a thread wherever I pleased, and where no one with a whip could have driven him'.

There was no doubt about the policy the missionaries were to follow. 'Let the people see what sort of men you are', they were told by Zinzendorf, 'and then they will be forced to ask "Who makes such men as these?".' The missionary was to 'exist as an example'. The pattern of his life was to be *missionary* in itself. His

[1] K. G. Hamilton, *John Etwein*, p. 29.
[2] E.g., *Instructions for Missionaries to the East* (1736); *Instructions to all Missionaries* (1738); *The Right Way to Convert the Heathen* (1740); *Homily for all Missionaries to Tranquebar* (1759).

preaching was to be driven home and the heathen convinced of the saving power and the fellowship of the Lamb by the living daily witness of the Moravian 'warrior'. The missionary must teach the heathen the dignity of labour by fending for himself and earning his own living. In the days of Zinzendorf, the missionary received from the Church just sufficient money to take him to the port of departure. Often the missionary walked to the port and then worked his passage across the ocean. On the mission field he took up whatever occupation would provide him with the bare amount of food and clothing. On 30 March 1756, Solomon Schumann wrote from Surinam: 'Brother Kamm is picking coffee; Brother Wenzel is mending shoes; Brother Schmidt is making a dress for a customer; Brother Doerfer is digging the garden; Brother Brambly is working on the canal.' 'We must banish all care as to how we shall live', said Henry Cossart, 'and I can say, to the praise of my Saviour, that I have received so many proofs of His sympathizing care in these matters, that I am not at all concerned about our maintenance in the future.' But the discipline was strict: 'If you take a penny more than you need', Zinzendorf told George Schmidt, 'I will dismiss you from the service.'

'You must never try to lord it over the heathen', the Count instructed the missionaries, 'but rather humble yourself among them, and earn their esteem through the power of the spirit'. When he officiated at the wedding of a Christian Negress in St Thomas, in accordance with the custom, Zinzendorf kissed the bride. The missionary must seek nothing for himself; no seat of honour, no report of fame. Like the cab-horses in London, the Count said, he must wear blinkers and be blind to every danger and to every snare and conceit. He must be content to suffer, to die and be forgotten.[1] During the life-time of Zinzendorf, no missionary biographies were allowed to be published. But there was no lack of volunteers for this noble army. 'When the Congregation heard the news that the witnesses in St Thomas had fallen asleep', Spangenberg tells us, 'all were full of desire to venture their lives also, and if I had asked for volunteers to go to that pestilential hole,

[1] Hutton, *op. cit.*, p. 177.

twenty or thirty Brethren and Sisters would have gone at once.'[1]

Although he affirmed the primary task of the missionary to be the preaching of the Lamb, confirming the unity of all men in him, and 'leading the heathen in the way of peace', Zinzendorf did not fail to encourage the moral growth and civil improvement of the converts. And in this the missionaries were outstandingly successful. They brought a discipline not only into the spiritual life of the heathen, but into their civil and social life as well. They were alive to Zinzendorf's timely warning: 'Let the heathen once taste European vices, and they will rush headlong to perdition.' None were to come to value the work of the Moravians more highly than the Governments of the lands where they laboured. The officials in Paramaribo urged them to preach to the slaves; their converts in Greenland were greatly admired by the Danish authorities; Sir Hugh Pallisser contributed to their mission in Labrador; and George Washington praised their services to the Red Indians. The missionaries did not meddle in party politics. By their example they taught the heathen to fear God and honour the King. 'Have you seen my castle?' the Governor of St Thomas asked Spangenberg. 'There it is', the Governor continued, pointing to the Moravian plantation, 'there is the cause of safety on this island. If that plantation were not there, I dare not sleep a night outside the fort.'[2]

The missionaries healed the sick; in their schools the heathen first studied the geography of their land, learned the simple trades, and read the Scriptures in their native tongue. The converts were taught to care for the sick and aged, for the widow and orphan. In Greenland old-age pensions were introduced. In St Thomas the negroes were trained to give to the poor-box and buy their own candles for the evening meetings. When the Eskimos heard of the suffering and losses of the Indian Congregation in the massacre at Gnadenhutten in Pennsylvania, they were eager to help. 'I have a fine reindeer skin which I will give,' said one. 'And I', said another,

[1] C. T. Ledderhose, *The Life of Augustus Gottlieb Spangenberg* (London, 1855), p. 56.
[2] Hutton, *op. cit.*, p. 498.

'will send them a seal, that they may have something to eat and burn.' Thus did Zinzendorf's Moravians spread the ecumenical conscience.

Zinzendorf's conception of the missionary, his message and strategy, was the first coherent contribution to the vast enterprise of Christian missions in the modern era. His genius and leadership gave an undoubted impetus to the other churches to plan their Christian witness in terms of the globe. There was direct Moravian influence in the foundation of both the Basel and the Leipzig Missionary Societies. The Methodist missionary enterprise followed the Moravian path. It is certain that the London Missionary Society received direct guidance from the Moravians: one of the founders, Rowland Hill, had been in correspondence with the Moravian Peter Brown of Antigua for over ten years. David Brogue, another founder, declared that the Moravians had excelled 'the whole Christian world' in missionary labours. Other leaders brought the Moravian journal, *Periodical Accounts* (first published in 1790 and still the oldest existing missionary magazine) to the preparatory meetings and derived their arguments from the Moravian experiences. When the LMS had been founded in 1795, the leaders directed inquiries to Christian Ignatius La Trobe, the Moravian secretary for missions, concerning the Moravian missionary recruitment and methods; and La Trobe replied in great detail. But the scene to which the historians of Christian missions turn again and again is that in the house of Mrs Beely Wallis on an October day in 1792 at Kettering. Before the little company of Baptists gathered there, William Carey threw down on the table copies of *Periodical Accounts* and exclaimed: 'See what these Moravians have done! Can't we Baptists at least attempt something in fealty to the same Lord?' And thus the Baptist Missionary Society was born.

The Ecumenical Vision

Zinzendorf hoped beyond hope that the unity of the churches he had preached for a life-time would come in embryo on the mission field and flower across the whole of Christendom. Denominationalism on the mission field had no place in his calculations. 'In Europe', he said, 'our divisions are rooted in necessity and love, but there is no sense let alone Christianity, in carting the stuff to America.' 'It pains me', he wrote, 'to see people polishing up the Churches again for the heathen and asking them to which of the Christian Denominations they belong.'[1] 'You must not enrol your converts as members of the Moravian Church', he instructed the missionaries, 'you must be content to enrol them as Christians.' The supreme aim of the Moravian missionary was not to make proselytes or win the largest possible multitude of candidates for baptism, but rather that the fellowship of the Lamb and the light of his Gospel should shine everywhere. One fact illustrates both the denominational poverty and the ecumenical riches of the Moravian Church. In 1736 Frederick Martin gained 700 converts in the West Indies; he baptized only thirty into the Moravian Church.

The other Moravian leaders learned this irenic and ecumenical lesson from Zinzendorf and honoured his strategy. 'We never enter into controversy with any other Denomination', wrote Bishop Spangenberg, 'nor do we attempt to win over to our Church any of the heathen who are already in connection with those of another Church.' Bishop Ettwein, the Moravian missionary and statesman in North America, declared: 'If the fruit is but brought to Him, to whom it belongs, no matter, whether the reapers be Moravians, Episcopalians, Presbyterians or Baptists etc.'[2] There were others, too, not of Zinzendorf's flock, who appreciated the wise foresight of his strategy. When Henry Cossart visited Rome in 1758 he told the Pope that 'Moravian missionaries do not teach the heathen the differences that keep the Church at home apart, but only the incarnation of God in Christ, the meritorious life, suffering and death of Jesus the Saviour, till the Holy Spirit enters their hearts with his gracious power. That is the work of our unity in all the earth.' The Pope was greatly pleased and laying his hand on the Moravian's head, he said, 'Our blessing be with you and the people to whom you belong.'[3]

[1] Baudert, *op. cit.*, p. 398.   [2] Hamilton, *op. cit.*, p. 95.
[3] S. H. Gapp in *World Dominion*, vol. xi, no 4, p. 411.

Still today the divided Church faints for the realization of Zinzendorf's dream, but to say that is not to minimize the denominational co-operation in mission affairs which has arisen from such ecumenical inspiration.[1]

Zinzendorf's conception of the relationship between the Christians at home and the native Christians in the mission field was that of a partnership of obedience, in the unity and fellowship of Christ. The terms 'sending and receiving countries', even 'older and younger churches', would have been abhorrent to him. He was swift to recognize the diversity of racial and individual gifts, and from the beginning he insisted on the enlistment of native 'Helpers' wherever possible. 'Zinzendorf made it a practice to give recently converted Indians', wrote Ettwein, 'the offices of teachers, elders, etc.'[2] 'It would be much better', wrote Zinzendorf, 'if there were men of their own nation among the Hottentots and other heathen, who could take care of their own people; for as soon as we send people there, the heathen remain subject to the Europeans.' Where the situation could best be served by it Zinzendorf permitted the introduction of the Herrnhut organization and discipline, but in general he was against 'applying the Herrnhut yardstick'; and always the natives were encouraged to take responsibility. A native Helper was stationed at Tappus in St Thomas; the Helper Peter was appointed Chief Elder of the brethren, and the Helper Magdalene served as Chief Eldress of the sisters. In the pastoral visitation and in the individual care of souls at the 'Speaking', the assistance and witness of the Helpers were of immeasurable value

[1] From many examples we may select the following. In the official *Diary* of the Moravians in Philadelphia, Pa., it is noted 'March 24th, 1743. Two Presbyterians were present and a Popish priest'. The London Association in Aid of Moravian Missions was founded in 1817 by Anglicans and members of other denominations because 'the fruits of their labours (Moravian) have excited wonder and gratitude in every Christian heart' (*First Report*, 1819, p. 7). In 1956, a theological college was opened at Kongwa, near Dodoma, Tanganyika, with a Moravian missionary as the principal, and an Anglican missionary as the vice-principal. The question which the African students ask of each other is not 'To which Denomination do you belong?' but 'Are you a Christian?' (*Moravian Messenger*, July 1957, p. 23).

[2] Hamilton, *op. cit.*, p. 104.

to the mission and the missionary. As soon as possible, hymns, litanies, parts of the Bible and the Catechism were introduced in the native tongue.

It was the total commitment of the Moravian Church to the cause of missions by Zinzendorf that makes him a guiding figure in the advancing ecumenical movement of today. Church and mission, he persistently affirmed, belong together. The General Synod of 1857 summed up his position: 'There never will be a Unity of the Brethren without a Mission to the Heathen, or a Mission of the Brethren which is not the affair of the whole Church as such. The Missions do not belong to themselves, nor yet to a Society, nor even a portion of the Brethren's Church, but to the whole Brethren's Unity.' The Moravian Church has always been a mission Church and not just the foster-mother of missionary societies.

As we watch the single-hearted, brave and singing followers of Zinzendorf, in their plain homespun clothes and quaint three-cornered hats, go voyaging across the oceans, we are witnessing not only a band of Christians who, as Melvill Horne wrote, 'have laboured, and suffered, and effected more than all of us',[1] but also 'a new phenomenon in the expansion of Christianity—an entire community of families as well as of the unmarried, devoted to the propagation of the faith'.[2] The ensign—a Lamb passant with a flag in a blood coloured field—fluttered from their little two-masted ships and proclaimed Christ's mission to the world. The modern ecumenical voyage had begun.

[1] E. A. Payne, *The Church Awakes* (London, 1942), p. 98.
[2] K. S. Latourette, *A History of the Expansion of Christianity*, vol. iii, p. 47.

6

THE APOSTLE OF UNITY

The Invisible Church

As in all things for Zinzendorf, the Lamb of God is the only ground of Christian unity. Again and again in his speeches and writings, Zinzendorf sought for words to make this point clear in its grand simplicity. In one of the Discourses preached at Marienborn and Herrnhaag in 1747, he tells how men have sought for 'the Hinge or chief point' common to all Christian teaching and persuasions, 'one at this, another at that Corner of the Body of Divinity'; how some have conscientiously embraced one of the 'so many different Platforms' and gained the name of 'religious' and yet have remained 'an enemy to the true Lord and God, neither able to understand nor relish what is most valuable in the Scriptures, and when brought in His way, shun the sight of it'. Zinzendorf continues:

'Tis therefore a concern which the whole world ought to lend their attention to settle, and all Christian People have a conference together upon, what is the inmost result and centre of that Religion so universally received, and deriving its name from Christ? what here is that object, which the eye ought to fasten, yea all the desire of the soul employ itself upon, for time and eternity? Now we simply declare 'tis no other than to view that transaction and posture of our God, when *He bled to death for our sins upon the Cross*. When our Hearts are struck by this, 'tis the beginning of an universal kind of Religion, disengaged from all debates, and where even a child soon becomes a Divine. The tenderest connection with our Redeemer, burying our corruption and misery in His death, is the great affair, and other things are regarded only for, and according to, the habitude they bear to this.[1]

As soon as the soul discovers this truth, says Zinzendorf, 'it reads the texts, it hears the sermon, it sings the hymn, and thinks it hears them for the first time in all its life:

> The Saviour's blood and righteousness
> It's fin'ry and wedding-dress
> Wherewith it may before God stand.

Thus the Denominations of the Christian religion, thus the human souls in them, shall be united.'[2]

These souls, dispersed throughout the world and in all the denominations, who have been washed in the Blood of the Lamb, who have been 'christed in his Heart',[3] who are of Christ's own flesh and bone and spirit, these are they who compose the Church Universal, the great Invisible Church of Christ, the Kingdom of his Cross, and are 'all held fast in His arms'.[4] And, according to Zinzendorf, it is the task of the ecumenical apostolate to make this Invisible Church of Christ visible or manifest in all its unity and glory on earth by bringing all the scattered children of God, the 'christed souls', 'into the Ark of holy Christendom (which is not this or that outward Congregation, but to be in the Ark means to attain to the same Spirit and Ideas of Heart with his true people, even though the person still abide in his former Dwelling-Place)'.[5] The line of Christian unity is not towards an organic union of all the denominations; but towards a unity, transcending all ecclesiastical divisions, of those souls who dwell in the Lamb and who cleave to one another in the 'unity of His wounds'. This ultimate unity in Christ is the unity which determines all other kinds of unity. Any part of its realization is an earnest of the final oneness of the Church in and with Christ, the 'Parent of the New Creation . . . the Restorer of things that were ruined and perished'.[6]

---

[1] *Maxims*, pp. 256-7.
[2] *Nine Public Discourses*, preached in Fetter Lane Chapel at London (1748), p. 120.
[3] *Ibid.*, p. 127.   [4] *Maxims*, p. 353.   [5] *Ibid.*, p. 357.   [6] *Maxims*, p. 343.

The unity of the true children of God, says Zinzendorf, is not a matter of the intellect, of creed, of ritual, of order, nor indeed of service in the first place but of the heart. The soul's union or fellowship with the Lamb is 'such a profession as cannot be taken up any more by education, but must be grounded on the testimony and sense of one's own heart, that he has sprung out of the pierced heart of Jesus, been hewn out of His side, and that the mouth of the Lamb has kissed him, and hallowed him with an indelible mark'.[1] In a discourse at Marienborn in 1747, Zinzendorf described this *Herzens-Religion* which provided instant recognition and fellowship to all the true Children of God:

When some thousands of men in different parts of the earth, of different languages, and who have never seen one anothers' faces, have yet one language in respect of the heart, and can listen to what is said even by a child if it but touch their favourite string; this convinces thinking people, that there is a *Religion of the Heart* where men's spirits harmonise together through His operations who can speak without outward sounds. . . . Of such a Religion or Confession (never to be learnt but through experience) we grant our Saviour to have been the Founder. How does He open and begin His lectures? Forget the glosses you have collected while you did not yet know the drift of Scripture, which is purely to send you to Me. Desist from that speculating method which leaves you ever hollow and empty, so that at last your tongue cleaves to the roof of your mouth; and let your first work be to eat. Do but look after Me, as a child does after the breast, and I will refresh you, and you shall thrive.[2]

Wherever these children of God meet, says Zinzendorf, in twos or threes or in a congregation, there is apparent amongst them 'a certain Signature which constantly carries in it a Compunction of the noblest kind, that has once arisen in their inward man by looking at the Crucified One. It is apparent that this is the Life of their Heart, and that it has been quite melted thereby.'[3]

'The Church of Christ', said Zinzendorf, 'is as yet scattered abroad, and not existing in any one seat, so as to be circumscribed

---

[1] *Ibid.*, p. 156.   [2] *Ibid.*, pp. 224–5.   [3] *Maxims*, p. 102.

there.'[1] 'No one must think', he emphasized repeatedly, 'that the Invisible Church, or People of God in every Nation (can) properly be tied to any one Party of Christians alone.'[2] The Lamb's People may come yea 'from among the erroneous Sects and in the darkest Ages; which however does not imply that all Religions are saving, or all Doctrines alike, but only that souls belonging to the Saviour are still preserved right in what is essential to Salvation'; the Lamb is the 'invisible Head, conversing and holding communion with these His members'.[3] Zinzendorf reflects in one of the *Explanatory Lectures* 'how many souls there are besides in the world, whom we never come to see in this life, yea who have never been under any powerful ministry at all, but have only perhaps once heard a short saying out of the Bible, a comfortable verse of an old hymn, and been forced to support themselves therewith all their life-time; often under great darkness and difficulties, but yet always with such a heart, as (tho' none around them might take notice of it) would directly manifest its gracious character upon meeting with another child of God? These compose that great Invisible Church of Christ, which is all held fast in His Arms.'[4] The Last Day shall come, says Zinzendorf, when the 'world shall see, how much wheat He still has: those lovers of Him and of mankind, who have almost wept their eyes out on account of human misery, shall be surprised at it. This is the Invisible Church.'[5]

The Denominations

As Bishop Baudert has written, Zinzendorf saw clearly that all the denominations, 'all these *ecclesiae visibiles,* which fought for their sole validity in a way that had little Christianity about it, had only a relative value, and could be only meant to point to the *ecclesia invisibilis*'.[6] But Zinzendorf had little interest in ecclesiastical joinery as such. His heart burned for the unity of the children of God, but he had no immediate wish for an organic union which would dispense with the denominations. In 1743 he said: 'The

---

[1] *Ibid.,* p. 139. [2] *Ibid.,* p. 205. [3] *Ibid.,* pp. 210–11.
[4] *Ibid.,* p. 353. [5] *Ibid.,* p. 39. [6] *Op. cit.,* p. 398.

Saviour has a hand in the fact that there are so many Sects (Denominations), and even if one had it in his power to diminish them by a single Sect, one ought first to ask whether it would be right to do it.' Zinzendorf observed that 'each Denomination is generally possessed of some Jewel (a clearness of Truth, or valuable Temper) peculiar to itself'.[1]

His recognition of the value of the denominations arose from a conception fundamental to Zinzendorf's ecumenical, missionary and educational thought and practice: the manifoldness of life.[2] A Moravian asked, 'Is not this the greatest unity—to agree that souls think differently?' 'Yes,' the Count replied, 'that is the real bond of unity.' 'Nature is full of different creatures of different inclinations,' said Zinzendorf; 'it is the same in the spiritual world; we must regard variety of thought as something beautiful.' He often remarked that 'there are as many religions (i.e. religious insights) as there are believing souls'. Therefore, he argued, souls must not be 'forced'; we must not expect them all to be measured by the same yardstick or to share exactly the same development of inward experiences.[3] 'God sees according to His infinite wisdom, how to deal with every soul,' said Zinzendorf; 'the manner, occasions and times are so different that they cannot be determined.' 'It is not gospel-like to prescribe rules, methods and dispositions, or require an equality of souls. We must leave all that to the free Grace of the Redeemer, how He may and will lay hold of souls.'[4] 'Our Saviour is not tied to anything'; how he gets hold of a soul 'remains still a mystery between them'.[5]

It was this rich variety in souls and in the approaches of the Lamb to them that led Zinzendorf to value the denominations: they were clear evidence of God's patience and of his loving care in providing different channels for the different temperaments and needs of his children. 'That is no harm', the Count declared, 'that men have Confessions of Faith, it is no harm that they are divided into religious Denominations.' And again he asserted, 'in the diversity of religious Denominations lies a divine Wisdom, which

[1] *Maxims*, p. 332.   [2] Baudert, *op. cit.*, p. 393.   [3] Baudert, *op. cit.*, p. 393.
[4] Berlin *Discourses* (1740), p. 29.   [5] Fetter Lane *Discourses*, pp. 50 and 42.

no particular person must disturb'.[1] No man must be censured 'in his Form, in his method of treating souls, and in the Outward Appearance of his Worship'; for 'everything has its own proper Form outwardly, its outward Shape, and one Thing cannot look as the other does; for every man has not the same manner of conception as another has, and hereby he distinguishes himself innocently and without offence'.[2] Again and again Zinzendorf repeated that 'the different established Religions (Denominations) are rather a divine than a human invention', and he believed that 'there is ground to think that there are National Religions; I mean, that some nations will never prosper, but under such and such an ecclesiastical constitution; and particularly, when at the Reformation some lands became Lutheran, and others Calvinist, that this was directed by Providence'.[3]

'No lightmindedness has any room in the matter of the religious Denominations', Zinzendorf told the Moravians at Fetter Lane in 1746. Because the differences in the denominations 'are something venerable, and contain a divine wisdom', he did not approve of 'anyone rashly quitting his former Persuasion' nor of anyone lightly attempting to win over other Church-members to his own denomination. Proselytizing had no place at all in Zinzendorf's ecumenical vocabulary. 'I despise everyone', he said, 'who without the deepest and best-digested reason goes over from one Denomination into another . . . nothing sounds so ridiculously in my ears as a Proselyte . . . it is a great trouble and pain for me to meddle or make with such a person, when I come to know he has left his former Denomination, especially among Protestants, who all take the Scripture as a rule of faith.'[4] And again, he said at Fetter Lane, 'he who in his heart is not disposed to tolerate, who is fond of forcing other people into his own notions and modes of worship; yea, who is only forward, when it may be done at a cheap rate, to take other people over into his own manner of worship; he shows thereby that he is no wise child of God, and is not endowed with the right spiritual understanding'.[5]

[1] *Maxims*, p. 205.   [2] Fetter Lane *Discourses*, p. 124.   [3] *Maxims*, p. 332.
[4] Fetter Lane *Discourses*, p. 125.   [5] *Ibid.*, p. 1.

Because each denomination 'is generally possessed of some Jewel peculiar to itself', it is the duty of each member of a denomination, argued Zinzendorf, to be as devoted a member as he can possibly be.[1] It is thus that other denominations can learn that same 'Excellence'. 'He that has attained a right insight, where the Excellence and wholesome solidity of his Form or System lies', said Zinzendorf in another *Explanatory Lecture*, 'and is faithful to it, can give his profession a lustre before all unprejudiced fellow-Christians, so that they must say, "In *that* respect we ought to learn of those people".'[2] It was not an 'ecumenical minimum' that Zinzendorf sought for in the enterprise of Christian unity, but a mutual respect, a sharing and co-operation in the common calling of the Christian mission. Condemnation, he said in 1744, 'is a tenet of melancholy minds'; 'it is the mark of a vulgar, mean disposition of mind, for people of one religious Denomination to take pleasure in embroiling those of another, or upon that account to shew virulence at each other'.[3] All denominations, like all periods of Church history, he was fond of saying, 'have two handles, and must be viewed on the good side to yield satisfaction'.[4]

Recognizing then that 'in the Diversity of religious Denominations lies a divine wisdom which no particular person must disturb', Zinzendorf was still insistent to proclaim that the denominations, as at that time constituted, had only a relative validity and served only to point faintly to the great Invisible Church of Christ. Indeed, he declared, these 'Denominations are called visible Churches of Christ' only because 'there are many worthy and living members of His amongst them, mixed with more that are not such'.[5] When Zinzendorf said that the denominations are

---

[1] 'I rebuked severely those light-minded young clergymen among the Lutherans, who ridiculed the ceremonial part of their duty (a Fashion very common at that time) and told them they should not turn *Scurrae* of holy things, which was to me an abomination. If they were not convinced that Ceremonies, however plain and few, were of service and fitting, they should leave them unused; should neither comply with them, nor mock them.' Zinzendorf's *An Exposition* (London, 1755), pt. ii, p. 10.
[2] *Maxims*, p. 333.   [3] Fetter Lane *Discourses*, p. 124.   [4] *Maxims*, p. 149.
[5] *Maxims*, p. 332.

rather a Divine than a human invention, he added: 'and in themselves, are not the Babel some have supposed.'[1] The operative words
are 'in themselves'; for it was evident to Zinzendorf, as it is so
evident to us today, that men have made a Babel of the denominations. And here for Zinzendorf arose the very head of the scandal of
disunity in Christendom. The greatest barrier to Christian unity
was not the division into the different denominations, but the
anomalous mixture and the lack of demarcation between the true
children of God ('wrapt in the Saviour') and the nominal Christians
within the denominations themselves. The deeper unity in the
Lamb was marred and hidden by a sham unity of nomenclature and
architecture. And the gravamen of the whole scandal lay in the
irony that it was the nominal Christians who most securely broke
the deeper unity of Christendom by their bigoted insistence on the
niceties of doctrine, the fashions of ritual and the contours of ecclesiastical constitutions.

Zinzendorf was the most irenic of souls, slow to anger and to
defend himself against the most malicious accusations, but a fierce
mixture of pity and indignation was aroused in him by the injury
done to the 'Body of Christ' through the pride, denominational
bigotry and self-deluding ignorance of the nominal Christians—
those who are 'flattered into a belief that they are good Christians
because they are good church-men'.[2] 'Now in these times', wrote
Zinzendorf, 'it is much worse and more difficult to love those
people, that presume to say that Christ is the Son of God, and yet
live in the utmost carelessness. They perform the outward ceremonies and duties of religion, but in reality deny the truth of it, or
betray their infidelity by their life and conversation.'[3] Such persons
'pretend to have to do with God', but 'who when they hear the
Saviour preached, regard it not otherwise, than if they were reading
a newspaper'.[4] These false Christians cling to 'the empty straw of
reason' and 'give themselves the trouble to be always representing
our religion as demonstrable to Reason'.[5] They take their stand on
morality and on self-righteousness, which Zinzendorf regarded

---

[1] *Ibid.*, p. 332.   [2] Hagen, *Old Landmarks*, p. 74.   [3] Berlin *Discourses*, p. 142.
[4] Fetter Lane *Discourses*, p. 86.   [5] *Ibid.*, p. 129.

'properly as one thing' with Deism. The Count argued that 'the most accomplished person both in understanding and morals is never the nearer' to true Christianity.[1] 'The word of the Cross', said Zinzendorf, 'is really too high for human reason, while it has the appearance of being too low.'[2] 'Christ's agony shews the heinousness of sin, and for ever puts an end to all purification by our own strength.'[3] A false good taste has also misled even so-called Christians to be ashamed of their Saviour: 'it is certainly very seldom that men of parts, authority, power and other qualities make frequent mention of our Saviour'.[4] Likewise 'all meditations upon the Godhead, upon that Almighty Being, upon that original loving Being, yea upon the virtuous and wonderful life of our Saviour Himself, when He is in our thoughts and minds, as the Son of God, as God of God, and Light of Light, quite orthodoxly, and as the Truth really is', are little worth to a man unless they are rooted in 'our Saviour's appearing before his heart in His suffering Form'; without such an appearing, all these things are 'nothing more, than a refined reasonable *Methodismus*, a small lift above pure Morality'.[5]

The simple truth, Zinzendorf concludes, is that these nominal Christians of all varieties do not 'adhere to Jesus as the Lamb of God'. They have no close intimacy with him nor with his Christians; any true Christian unity is at an end among them. Such people are in that extraordinary case of being able 'to speak of heavenly and divine things, without having experienced them in their hearts'.[6] Some even 'may adopt this Christian notion without a Christian experience of heart, and crudely glory in a Saviour they have never laid hold of';[7] but still they are without life spiritually and their stench is an offence and a hindrance to the Christian witness and unity.

Likewise, Zinzendorf declared, a denomination may lose her life if a nominal Christianity invades her totally: 'the moment her spirit is gone, and the body is without life, it must be dissolved and lose its Form also; those Church-bodies, which are not dissolved when life is wanting, either never had it, but were statues;

[1] *Maxims*, p. 239.   [2] *Ibid.*, p. 9.   [3] *Ibid.*, p. 346.   [4] Berlin *Discourses*, p. 9.
[5] Fetter Lane *Discourses*, p. 110.   [6] *Ibid.*, p. 76.   [7] *Maxims*, p. 318.

or if they had, then they are carcasses in the sight of God, till their figure likewise drops'.[1]

It was these considerations which led Zinzendorf to insist again and again that to be the member of a denomination was not at all one and the same thing as being one of the Flock of the Lamb, a member of his Church. A man, he argued, may say 'I am of Calvin's mind! still rather (according to my sentiments) may he say, I am of Luther's! But this gives neither the one nor the other the least right to salvation.'[2] Such a man may have 'read the Doctrine of Jesus, often heard lectures on it, so that he is able to relate it again, so that he is grounded in its principles according to his own Denomination; we can let such an one pass for nothing more than one of the so-called nominal Christian-people'.[3]

> And His Church stands as she hath stood,
> Jehovah's Father is her God,
> She still retaineth her first Dress,
> The Saviour's Blood and Righteousness.[4]

The true member of the Lamb's Church is one 'who will have no Wisdom, no Divinity, but that which arises only out of the Death and Sufferings of our Saviour, and has its foundations alone on His merits and blood'.[5] The true Christian is one of those who 'have experienced the power of the Death of Jesus on their hearts'.[6] He is one who can say 'He stands before my eyes as if I saw Him crucifying'; one to whom the Lamb is 'the true element in which the Children of God subsist';[7] one who has 'an inseparable friendship with the Lamb, the slaughtered Lamb';[8] and in the words which Zinzendorf was so fond of using, the true Christian is 'he that can say to Jesus, My Bone! I am flesh of His flesh, and bone of His bone; I am called Christian, because I am taken out of Christ,

---

[1] *Ibid.*, p. 91.   [2] *Ibid.*, p. 205.

[3] Fetter Lane *Discourses*, p. 127. Zinzendorf liked the distinction which the German language made between *ein Christ*, conveying his idea of the 'christed' member of Christ's Flock, and *ein Christianer*, a word analogous to the names of sects.

[4] Fetter Lane *Discourses*, p. 125.   [5] *Ibid.*, pp. 37–38.   [6] *Ibid.*, p. 8.

[7] *Ibid.*, p. 134.   [8] *Ibid.*, p. 162.

because I belong to Christ, because I am one spirit with Him'.[1] The ecumenical argument comes full circle: as soon as two persons of different denominations come together in the Lamb, 'and have one Heart, nothing can keep them from being agreed'.[2] When by faith and love we 'enter into our Saviour in such a manner, that we can no longer see or hear anything else above or beyond Him', then it is 'that we and Him remain in an indissoluble union together'.[3]

One main impulse of the ecumenical task, according to Zinzendorf, was a deep sense of repentance and need of forgiveness because that in the visible life of the churches or denominations, the holiness, the apostolicity and the unity the Church had been broken by the narrowness, bigotry and pride of nominal Christianity. It was the ecumenical task to manifest more clearly the true nature of the Church of Christ by bringing together in some 'field of encounter' those 'christed souls', within and outside the denominations, who are already at one with Christ and with one another in the 'unity of His wounds' and in the Invisible Church. This unity must be made visible to all the denominations and to all the world. Such a manifestation would not dissolve the denominations, but would serve to purge and strengthen them in their witness to the Lamb; and it would face all the churches with the radical change that would take place in their life and work if they were consistent with the belief that the unity we have 'in Christ' is far more important than our differing interpretations of his will.

The Renewed Moravian Church

It was a vital foundation stone of Zinzendorf's ecumenical vision and enterprise that, because the Lamb is one with his Church, the unity of the Church is a fact to be built on and realized, rather than an ideal to be achieved. The unity of the 'christed ones' in all the world already exists: it has to be rediscovered and made visible. How then, asked Zinzendorf, could this be done in the Christendom of his day with its proud divisions? More particularly,

[1] *Ibid.*, p. 9. [2] Fetter Lane *Discourses*, p. 99. [3] *Ibid.*, p. 168.

what part could the Moravians play in this grand task? The simple answer to this question is that the Moravians were to serve the cause of Christian unity through the development of Zinzendorf's *Diaspora* and *Tropus* conceptions. These were evolving conceptions and they will form the theme of the next two chapters. But in preparation, we must attempt briefly to indicate the development of the community at Herrnhut into the Renewed Unitas Fratrum or Moravian Church, with her own full ministerial orders restored and recognized by the civil and ecclesiastical authorities: for within this development lies the explanation of Zinzendorf's view of the ecumenical mission of the Moravian Church.

There is no doubt that the descendants of the ancient Unitas Fratrum in Herrnhut longed for their Church to be fully revived and constituted. In 1727, Zinzendorf said of the Brethren: 'This little flock, which belongs to the Lord, shall be preserved as long as I live, and as far as my influence goes, after I am gone, till He comes.'[1] In 1741 his allegiance to all the churches in the cause of unity was made clear: 'I have been, and still am, associated with the Moravian Brethren . . . yet I do not separate myself from the Lutheran Church . . . I cannot restrict myself as a witness to one church, for all the earth is the Lord's, and all souls are his. I am debtor to all.'[2] In 1745 the singularity of the Moravian Church was uppermost in his mind: he declared that he could no more abolish the Moravian Church, nor do away with their bishops, nor put them out of existence and memory, than any one in Geneva or London or Berlin could surrender archives intrusted to them. But still in 1752 Zinzendorf could foresee the termination of the Moravian Church. He was in fact trying to reconcile what proved to be two incompatible ideals. On the one hand, he held the conviction that it was his God-given task to renew the ancient Unitas Fratrum; and on the other, his strong 'instinct of ecumenicity' drove him to discourage any denominational ambition or emphatic growth of the Unitas Fratrum (as renewed in the Moravian Church). Zinzendorf thought that he could combine the two ideals

[1] See F. Bovet, *The Banished Count*, p. 105.
[2] See J. R. Weinlick, *Count Zinzendorf*, p. 152.

by making the Moravian Church a servant of Christian unity in bearing the central *Herzens-religion* amongst all the denominations. By temperament and by conviction, Zinzendorf felt himself called to lead a society which would be a special agency of an evangelistic character to kindle, wherever hearts were ready, the flame of 'devotion to the Saviour' in the existing denominations. Thus the Moravians would implement the Pietist conception of *ecclesiolae in Ecclesia* by cultivating fellowship among the children of God in a network of societies within the established Churches. But the historical circumstances of the settlement of the Moravian refugees in Herrnhut, the position taken up by the State authorities, and the needs of the growing missionary adventures, led Zinzendorf to agree reluctantly to his planned society (*Gemeine*) being turned into a full-fledged church (*Kirche*) which came to be known as the Moravian Church.

The original status of the Herrnhut community was that of an *ecclesiola in Ecclesia*: it was a community within the Lutheran State Church in Saxony. As Dr Weinlick points out:

Though the Moravian refugees belonged to a previously existing Denomination, their continuance as such was not any more welcome to the German authorities than if they had been a sectarian split from the State Church. This confronted Zinzendorf with the delicate problem of satisfying both the authorities and the refugees. Under the restricted freedom of his day, it was only by keeping the Moravians close to the State Church that he won toleration for them. This he did by convincing the authorities that Moravians, despite their distinctive ways of worship and social arrangements, were loyal to the all-important Augsburg Confession. Had Zinzendorf allowed the refugees to become a Denomination immediately, they would have been promptly outlawed.[1]

The infant community was surrounded by a persistent and vigilant enmity. A host of pamphleteers attacked the Brethren, their itinerant preachers were fined and imprisoned, but the kernel of the opposition was directed against Zinzendorf himself. He was an enigma which teased and defeated both the reason and

[1] *Moravian Messenger* (London, May 1960), p. 8.

imagination of the civil and ecclesiastical authorities: he was a Count who mixed with and ministered to the humblest of men; he was a supposedly loyal son of the Lutheran Church and yet he aided such strange sects and separatists as the Schwenkfelders— he was even reported to have had correspondence with the Pope on the subject of a hymn-book for all Christians of every denomination! Both the Lutherans and the Pietists denounced Zinzendorf as a heretic and the founder of a new sect; the Saxon and Austrian landowners denounced him as an anarchist, seducing the peasants from their rightful service to their overlords. But envy was a root cause of this animosity. Zinzendorf was a zealous and unconventional Christian who longed for the unity of all the followers of Christ in an age of religious feudalism and apathy.

Zinzendorf had the complete courage of his convictions and he welcomed every inquiry. His immediate reaction to all criticism was 'Come and see!' The Imperial ambassador lodged a formal complaint at the Saxon Court against Zinzendorf and in January 1732 a commission from Dresden investigated the doctrine and discipline at Herrnhut. The commission left the Settlement well satisfied and with a great esteem for the congregation. But the problems mounted in Herrnhut. A second pastor was required but the Saxon Government forbade the appointment of Professor Steinhofer from Tübingen who was eager to accept the office. Zinzendorf himself was under attack for exercising the ministry of the Word without having been ordained. In March 1734 he went to Stralsund and submitted to a theological examination by two examiners from the University of Greifswald. On 26 April he was given a complete certificate of Lutheran orthodoxy. On 19 December he was formally recognized as a minister by the Faculty of Theology in Tubingen and on the same day he preached in the cathedral. Some at least of his enemies were now disarmed.

Events were now conspiring, much against the wishes of Zinzendorf, towards the revival of the ministerial orders of the ancient Unitas Fratrum, and hence towards the full renewal of that Church. Lawfully ordained ministers of the Brethren were urgently needed in the mission fields so that the Moravian baptisms and marriages and Communions could pass unchallenged.[1] At last it was agreed in Herrnhut and confirmed by the Lot that the Brethren should take over the episcopal succession of the ancient Unitas for the ordination of ministers. In 1735 this episcopal line was represented by two bishops: Daniel Ernest Jablonski, grandson of Comenius, who had been appointed bishop in 1699 and held this office along with his position as the Reformed Court Preacher in Berlin;[2] and Christian Sitkovius of Thorn in Poland who was Superintendent of the Reformed and Unity Congregations in that country and had been also consecrated a Bishop of the Unitas in 1734. The new bishop was to be David Nitschmann, the carpenter, a descendant of an old Unitas family in Moravia. The consecration took place in Jablonski's house in Berlin on Sunday, 13 March 1735. The persons present were Jablonski, Nitschmann and two members of the Bohemian congregation in Berlin who were invited as witnesses. Sitkovius sent his concurrence by letter. The revival of the episcopate appealed to the Brethren as a means of gaining secular recognition for their ministers with freedom to organize religious work. Above all it appealed to them as an outward and visible sign of the complete renewal of their ancient Church.[3]

Meanwhile the opposition to Zinzendorf was coming to a head. The Pietists resented his success; the Lutherans regarded him as a Separatist; the nobility (including his mother and aunt Henrietta) felt that he had disgraced their rank; and when Baron Huldenberg of Neukirch formally complained to Dresden that his vassals had been enticed from his service and joined to the fanatics at Herrnhut by Zinzendorf, the new King Frederick Augustus III of Saxony issued an edict of banishment—without right of appeal—against Zinzendorf on 20 March 1736. From 9 to 18 May 1736 another Commission of Inquiry, two nobles and two divines, investigated

---

[1] On the passage out to St Croix in 1733, the Brethren had chosen a 'deacon' for themselves, one Mathes Miksch, to teach and baptize.

[2] See Norman Sykes, *Daniel Ernst Jablonski and the Church of England* (London, 1950).

[3] It was not until 1745 that the orders of 'Presbyter' and 'Deacon' were introduced together with such other orders of the ancient Unitas as 'Acolouth' and 'Deaconess'.

in detail the doctrine and discipline at Herrnhut. The verdict was
the same as before: provided the members there remained peaceable
and conformed to the Augsburg Confession, they might remain
at Herrnhut; but no new members were to be added. Perhaps the
more subtle reason for the favourable report was that the rulers
of Saxony could ill afford to lose such skilled and industrious
workmen. But the edict against Zinzendorf remained firm: from
March 1736 until October 1747, except for a few months in 1737–
8, he was an exile and in literal truth the wandering minstrel of
the Lamb.

Step by step, during these years, despite the undenominational
emphasis of Zinzendorf, the Moravian Church was moving towards
a more definite recognition of her independence by the civil
authorities. King Frederick William of Prussia wrote to Jablonski
on 28 October 1736, that 'having now myself seen the Count of
Zinzendorf' he found him to be 'an honest and sensible man, who
hath no other views, but the propagation of true and solid Christianity'.[1] The King advised Zinzendorf to be consecrated as a
bishop of the Brethren. On 20 January 1737 Zinzendorf arrived in
London to seek the opinion of Dr John Potter, then Archbishop
Elect of Canterbury, on the validity of the Moravian episcopate.
Dr Potter gave him a most cordial welcome, urged him to be made
a bishop of the Brethren, and declared 'that the objections against
the Moravian Church were frivolous: that no Englishman, who
had any notion of Ecclesiastical History, could doubt their succession'.[2] On 20 May 1737, at Jablonski's house in Berlin, Zinzendorf was consecrated a bishop by Jablonski and Nitschmann, with
the concurrence by letter of Sitkovius. No service could have shown
forth more clearly the ecumenical spirit of the old and renewed
Unity. As an American Moravian scholar has written, 'A clergyman
of the Reformed Church consecrating a Lutheran to the episcopacy
of a third church is hardly conventional', yet it was 'prophetic of

[1] *Acta Fratrum*, p. 45.
[2] *Report* of the Committee appointed by the Archbishop of Canterbury to
consider the Orders of the Unitas Fratrum or Moravians (London, 1907),
p. 55.

what the Renewed Moravian Church was to become, both a denomination and a brotherhood of interdenominational status'.[1] That the consecration was approved, and indeed urged, by the King Frederick William, prepared the way for the official recognition of the Moravian Church in Prussia in 1742. On 15 December 1737, Zinzendorf carried out his first ordination, at Ronneburg. It was that of Peter Böhler, the adviser and inspirer of John Wesley.

Slowly even the King of Saxony had a change of heart. In 1747 he visited Herrnhut and in October of the same year he ended Zinzendorf's banishment. On the afternoon of 14 October, a Lovefeast of two hundred persons, including two Eskimos from Greenland, welcomed the Count back to Herrnhut. The wheel had come full circle. The King invited Zinzendorf to establish more settlements in Saxony, and after another Commission of Inquiry, a royal decree of 20 September 1749 granted the Brethren full liberty of conscience and worship in Saxony.

In the face of continued slander and opposition, Zinzendorf was eager for a thorough Parliamentary examination of the Brethren's position in England. In January 1749 he and his company prepared their plans, at Northampton House in fashionable Bloomsbury Square and at the country seat of Ingatestone hall about twenty miles from London. On 25 March 1749 leave was granted to bring in a Bill, drafted by White, the Brethren's counsel, 'for encouraging the people known by the name of Unitas Fratrum, or United Brethren, to settle in His Majesty's Colonies in America' (22 Geo. II cap. 30). Although there was at first some opposition to the Bill in the House of Lords led by the Lord Chancellor and Dr Sherlock, Bishop of London, it was passed without a division on 12 May. In particular Lord Granville and Lord Chesterfield spoke in favour of the measure. Although the Bill described the Brethren as an 'Episcopal Church', the bishops of the Anglican Church had already decided, at a meeting at Lambeth Palace held at Easter, not to oppose it. In the Lords debate, Dr Maddox, Bishop of Worcester, spoke forcibly in favour of the Bill. 'It will be an edification to myself', he said, 'and the whole episcopal bench, and all true

[1] J. R. Weinlick, *Count Zinzendorf*, p. 137.

Protestants of England, if the British nation expresses itself in favour of the Brethren; for whatsoever benefit England confers upon this ancient confessor Church, must be an encouragement to all Evangelical Christians throughout the world, to expect nothing but good from this country.'[1] At these words, 'Content' was cried out all over the House. On 6 June the *Acta Fratrum* received the King's signature. Henceforwards the Unitas Fratrum or Renewed Moravian Church was to be acknowledged throughout Great Britain and her dependencies as 'an ancient Protestant Episcopal Church, which has been countenanced and relieved by the Kings of England', to be descended through Comenius from the Bohemian Brethren, and to be a sister-church of the Church of England.[2]

The heritage of their fathers had now fallen in full measure upon that faithful Hidden Seed which had first taken so humble a refuge upon the estate of a nobleman in Saxony. And now we can look backwards and forwards to see these Brethren, led by Zinzendorf, further engaged upon the grand task of Christian unity.

[1] *Report* of the Archbishop's Committee, p. 58.
[2] See J. Taylor Hamilton, 'The Recognition of the Unitas Fratrum as an Old Episcopal Church by the Parliament of Great Britain in 1749', *Transactions of the Moravian Historical Society* (Bethlehem, Pa., 1925), Special ser., vol. ii, pt. 2, pp. 43 ff.

7

THE PILGRIM CONGREGATION
AND THE DIASPORA

———

The Itinerant Headquarters

As Zinzendorf saw it, the grand ecumenical task was to redis-
cover and to make visible the unity of the 'christed ones' in all
the world. As a contribution towards the fulfilment of this task,
the Brethren were to act as a leaven and as a servant to all the
churches. 'The Brethren', he wrote, 'have this hereditary principle,
that they gladly lend their assistance to any Protestant constitution, without ever affecting Dominion themselves. And their
endeavour is to cure the human disease from the bottom, and
promote that on which happiness essentially turns, without dis-
suading any one in other respects from the Form and Persuasion
he was of before.'[1]

To carry out this duty, Zinzendorf's fertile mind at first devised
two kindred ventures, within the *ecclesiolae in Ecclesia* framework,
for the Brethren: the Pilgrim Congregation (*Pilgergemeine* or
Pilgerhaus), and the Diaspora.

The word 'pilgrim' was always most dear to Zinzendorf and
went to the heart of his conception of a Christian and of the Church.
'He regarded it as a privilege', wrote Spangenberg, 'to be merely
a pilgrim on earth.' 'I have learnt by experience', said Zinzendorf,
'that there is happiness in being at home everywhere, as He was
who passed most of His life as a pilgrim and in exile.' It was almost
with joy that he received the news of the edict of banishment on

[1] *Maxims*, p. 125.

116

20 March 1736. 'The time has come', he declared, 'to gather the Pilgrim Congregation and to preach the Saviour to the whole world. Our home will be that place where at the moment our Saviour has most for us to do.'[1] And thus it was that for the ten years of exile at least, Zinzendorf and his inmates were literally strangers and pilgrims upon earth. He roamed the Continent, preaching and singing and planning in Wetteravia, Berlin, Switzerland, Holland and England—and wherever he went the Pilgrim Congregation went with him, in near-by lodgings or sharing his home, and all intent on building up the same kind of unity among all Christians.

The Pilgrim Congregation was the itinerant headquarters, training, organizing and manning a vast campaign of evangelism and ecumenical witness. No one who was not ready to go anywhere at any time for any purpose in the service of the Lamb could be a member of it. The personnel changed frequently as the 'warriors' came and went on their various missions; and its personnel derived from varying nations and denominations. One day in 1740 seven adherents were confirmed—a Pole, a Hungarian, a Swiss, an Englishman, a Swede, a Livonian and a German. The Pilgrim Congregation was made up from all ranks of society, but everyone shared the common hardships, the same food, the same few necessities. None received any wages; if a Pilgrim had private means he contributed to the common needs. The main burden of all the expenses was met by Zinzendorf out of his estate and by gifts and loans from Holland and other friendly sources. The Countess Zinzendorf was in charge of all the housekeeping, and Frederick de Watteville with Jonas Paulus Weiss helped her to manage the finances. Notable members of the Pilgrim Congregation in the early days were Christian David, John de Watteville, Leonard Dober, John Nitschmann and Wencelaus Neisser. An unending stream of visitors and correspondence flowed through the 'Pilgrim House', and a *Schreiber-Collegium* was soon set up to transcribe the letters and the *Diary* of meetings, discourses, conversations and events, which

[1] See Spangenberg, *Zinzendorf*, pp. 207–8.

kept the scattered Brethren in touch with one another on their various campaigns.

The daily round of services and the rules of Herrnhut were kept in the Pilgrim Congregation as it travelled around the Continent and the British Isles, but there was nothing sectarian about its activity. ''Tis a common opinion', said Zinzendorf in one of his discourses at Herrnhaag in 1741, 'that whoever is received into the Congregation, devotes his future life, and all that he has, to the said Congregation. But it is the least of my concern, whether such a one remains with us, or returns to the Religion (Denomination) he belonged to before. Let him only look upon the Lamb slain for us, as the most precious of all objects, and believe that we tenderly love Him, and let him seek to be of the same mind therein.'[1] It was no matter to which denomination an awakened soul belonged. A Pilgrim, according to Zinzendorf, was 'a Philadelphian (lover of the Brethren), with a Moravian coat and a Lutheran tongue'; his mission was to awaken the slumbering Christians in the different Churches and more effectively to 'clothe them, if they can, in their several religious habits, as Lutherans, Anglicans, Calvinists, Moravians'.[2] The Pilgrim Congregation claimed nothing for itself: it sought to be a candlestick in a dark world and amongst the churches.

One day at Tübingen, Zinzendorf was asked to state the best means of securing that fraternal communion, of which he spoke so much, amongst believers. 'Ah,' he replied, 'it is difficult to say, but it is easy to do.' And when surprise was expressed at this answer, he added, 'We have only to be as zealous in the cause of Jesus as the children of this world are in their affairs, and the communion of saints will be realised.' The Pilgrim Congregation, in all its enterprises and in its very being, was to be an example of that *koinonia*, that fellowship and unity, which comes to all Christians when they think less of clinging narrowly to their own denominations, and think more of cleaving simply to the Saviour and to one another in him.

[1] Gambold, *Maxims*, pp. 32–33.
[2] Daniel Benham, *Memoirs of James Hutton* (London, 1856), p. 118.

Messengers to Europe

The Pilgrim Congregation did not become a permanent feature of the Moravian Church, but the cognate conception of the Diaspora is still a flourishing factor in the Moravian ecumenical witness today. Foreshadowing the great protest of Kierkegaard (incidentally, educated in a Moravian school), Zinzendorf persistently pointed out the absurdity of identifying the Church of Christ simply with those men and women who took the name of 'Christian'; or indeed of identifying all true Christians simply with those who belonged to one or other of the denominations. He denounced the nominal Christian as a breaker of Christian unity. 'A heathen', he declared, 'can be more readily saved than a nominal Christian. The latter is in still greater danger of the judgment, because he provokes the wrath of God by neglecting his Christian privileges.'[1] God has his own in every denomination, said Zinzendorf, and the mission of the Diaspora was to increase the fellowship of all these 'dispersed' true Christians in all the churches; to 'gather together in one the children of God that were scattered abroad' (John 11.52); and to make visible 'that great Invisible Church of Christ, which all is held fast in His arms'.[2]

The work of the Diaspora began immediately after the pente-costal experience of unity on 13 August 1727, but Zinzendorf did not officially use the name until 1749. The name came from the original Greek of I Peter 1.1. 'Peter, an apostle of Jesus Christ to the elect strangers of the Diaspora of Pontus', that is, 'living scattered throughout Pontus.' Dr Weinlick is undoubtedly right when he says that 'this Diaspora was really Zinzendorf's first love'.[3] By means of it he saw the Moravian Church fulfilling her self-denying task of being a servant to all the Churches. It was through the network of meetings and societies established by the Diaspora in the various denominations that the Moravians quickened the life and unity of Christendom and justly earned the tribute of a Roman Catholic scholar: 'the Moravians can point to a time, not

---

[1] Hagen, *Landmarks*, pp. 109–10.
[2] *Maxims*, p. 353.   [3] *Count Zinzendorf*, p. 88.

above 200 years since, when they were the vital leaven of European Protestantism'.[1]

The Moravian itinerant messengers—they were not evangelists in the strict sense—of the Diaspora went out from Herrnhut as early as the autumn of 1727. They travelled in twos and threes. In September 1727, Gottlieb Wried and Andrew Beyer began their journey through Lichtenstein, Kalditz, Saalfield and Bayreuth. In Jena they aroused the interest of the young Spangenberg in Christian unity and the reality of Christian fellowship. In the same month, David Nitschmann and John Nitschmann were graciously received in Copenhagen by the Crown Prince Charles and his sister. They were much confused in the presence of Royalty. When John made his Spanish bow he fell full-length on the floor, struck the stove violently and scattered the firewood all over the room. But he did not sprawl for long before the Crown Prince. He got up from the floor with as much dignity as he could muster, and poured out his soul in testimony to the fellowship to be enjoyed by all men in the Lamb. On 3 April 1728 Zinzendorf sent John Toeltschig, David Nitschmann and Wencelaus Neisser on a deputation to England with letters to the University of Oxford, the SPCK, and the Countess Lippe-Schaumberg at the Court of George II. Within three years the Diaspora seed had been sown over a wide area of Europe—in Sweden, the Baltic Provinces, Austria, Berlin, Wurttemberg, Pomerania, the Palatinate and Switzerland. The area of influence widened as the years went by; in the Baltic Provinces alone, there came to be 45,000 persons attached to the Diaspora societies. At a Synod at Marienborn in 1745 a total of 159 societies were reported. Classified according to their Church affiliations, there were eighty-eight Lutheran, thirty-eight Reformed, thirty Moravian, and three unnamed. At a Synod at Zeist in 1746, it was reported that the Brethren's Church 'stood in connection' with 540 communities, not including the Baltic states.

Nor were the persecuted Brethren in Bohemia and Moravia forgotten. In 1728 Melchior Nitschmann and George Schmidt

[1] Knox, *Enthusiasm*, p. 390.

determined to visit the awakened Christians in Salzburg and to call upon the Brethren at Lititz on the same journey. But both were seized by the Catholics and shut up in the Schildberg prison. Schmidt remained a prisoner for six years, but Nitschmann died from the severe privations on 27 February 1729. His body was buried in a place reserved for heretics and criminals. Zinzendorf mourned his loss deeply; 'in him I have lost half my heart,' he declared.

Zinzendorf organized the work of the Diaspora on well-defined lines. Each 'missionary' or 'messenger' in the Diaspora had his own special district. He went from house to house and held meetings for prayer and exhortation. In all the Diaspora meetings, Zinzendorf ordered, there must be an emphasis on informality, simplicity, warmth and the open sharing of the joy and fellowship in the Lamb. No opportunity was to be given for the *odium theologicum*—a prime cause of division—to raise its head. 'The people', said Zinzendorf, 'should only sing, pray and talk with one another. What goes beyond the discussion of Christian experience is offensive. For with religious addresses without pastors the people bring much poorer goods to market than in the church, and therewith comes pride.' Some of the 'visited' remained just attenders and witnesses to Christian unity at the Diaspora meetings; but others were formed into Societies in close fellowship with the Moravian Church, reading Moravian literature and holding services on the Moravian pattern. These Society members, however, never shared in the Moravian Lord's Supper. They took this Sacrament in the State Church or the denomination to which they belonged and whose services they regularly attended. It was never intended by Zinzendorf that the Moravian Church herself should increase: only the spirit of Moravianism—the spirit of unity amongst all Christians.

The *Instructions* given to every Diaspora messenger were designed to avoid giving any occasion of offence to the other Churches.

1. Should any clergyman oppose the labours of the Brethren, visits to his parish must, for that time, be discontinued, for an attempt to continue these visits in direct opposition to him would be highly censurable.

2. When impediments are thus laid in our way, either by clergymen or magistrates, it is our duty to lay the case in prayer before the Saviour, and wait His time for removing them.
3. No assemblies of the Societies are to be held during the time of public service in the parish church, or late at night.
4. It is our duty to avoid all appearance of obtrusiveness, and what might attract useless notice.[1]

As always, the Moravians thought in terms of action, but they never sought to be other than 'the quiet in the land'.

Some of the clergymen of the Lutheran State Church objected to the work of the Diaspora and indeed an attempt was made to compel every candidate for holy orders to take an oath renouncing all intercourse with the Moravians. But the attempt failed. From 1754 and continuing for 117 years, an annual Ministers' Conference, with corresponding members in many parts of Europe, met at Herrnhut. The Conference was composed largely of ministers, teachers and ministerial candidates of the State Churches who, under the presidency of Zinzendorf or another Moravian minister, discussed the methods of propagating the Gospel and of encouraging the Diaspora purpose. These men, like many others, had learned the value of the Diaspora Societies in their own churches, and they combined to defeat any flagrant plot to hinder the Moravian work for unity.

As we watch the Pilgrim Congregation and the unpretentious messengers of the Diaspora quietly making their ecumenical and irenic witness across the highways and byways of Europe, we must always remember that Zinzendorf was not only the organizer of the whole endeavour but also an active warrior in the very front ranks. He asked no special favours or circumstances for himself. He was a rich noble, but he made long itineraries on foot, travelling incognito and living on such food as kindly disposed folks offered him. He had no press agents and he did not organize tent or tabernacle meetings. He regarded mass-meetings for evangelism as mobs or grand spectacles rather than agencies of the Lamb.

[1] John Holmes, *History of the Protestant Church of the United Brethren*, vol. ii, pp. 31–32.

He spoke to anybody, to peasants and nobles, to gypsies, beggars, to travellers on foot, on horse-back, in coach-and-four; he held devotional meetings in cottages and castles, in universities and hostels; and singing-services for himself and any of his company as they made their way through the land. He picked up orphans and helpless old people and arranged for them to be sent and to be cared for in Herrnhut.

Zinzendorf was early in the field of the Diaspora. In November 1727 he visited Prince Christian Ernst of Saalfield to discuss Christian unity. In the course of his journey he held informal meetings in Rudelstadt, Bayreuth and Coburg, and formed an *ecclesiola in Ecclesia* among a 'little band of believers' in the University of Jena. In 1728 he gathered both staff and students into 'a spiritual plantation' at Halle. In 1735 he held Diaspora services in Copenhagen and in the Swedish ports.[1] In July 1736 he set out for Livonia and prepared plans for an influential Diaspora work in Riva, Wolmar and in Reval, the capital of Estonia.[2] In the November he was given a great welcome in the city of Frankfort by the clergy and the State officials who encouraged the members of the State churches to attend his services. The Diaspora Society there attracted in later years the support of Susannah von Klettenberg, the friend of Goethe, whom he portrayed as the *schöne Seele* in *Wilhem Meister*.[3] In 1739 and 1742, Zinzendorf visited Switzerland and formed Diaspora Societies in Berne, Basel and Geneva—a city, he writes, 'hitherto so devoted to philosophy that it scarcely submitted to the ignominy of the Cross'.

Difficulties served only to quicken Zinzendorf's zeal and courage. When he was with the Pilgrim Congregation in Berlin in 1738 all the clergy opposed him and no church pulpit was open to him. Whereupon, with the support of King Frederick William, he threw his house open to the crowds which thronged to hear him. People of all classes and shades of belief came to the house-meetings; the

[1] See K. S. Latourette, *Christianity in a Revolutionary Age* (London, 1959), vol. i, p. 86, for the Moravian influence in Sweden.

[2] *Ibid.*, vol. ii, pp. 197–8, for the Moravian influence in Estonia.

[3] Goethe's mother was also a member of this Society, and the poet himself often attended the meetings.

men on Sundays and Wednesdays; the women on Tuesdays and Thursdays; and as many as forty-five carriages were to be seen drawn up outside the Count's door. The *Berlin Discourses* which he delivered at this time were published and ran through many editions.[1] Zinzendorf spoke with little preparation, but 'as soon as I begin to speak', he wrote, 'I feel the coals from the altar. I am sensitive to the varying moods of my hearers. They often shed tears, which is the case even with the soldiers among them. May the Saviour give permanence to what they feel.'

When Zinzendorf heard of the edict of banishment issued by the Empress Elizabeth against the Diaspora in Livonia, he set out immediately across the winter snows and the broken roadways for St Petersburg. On 23 December 1743 he arrived in Riga and there he was arrested and imprisoned in the city fortress. On Christmas Eve he wrote to the Countess: 'Here we are, a nice little band of prisoners for the Saviour . . . and I am sure the Saviour will arrange all things for the best.' He wrote to the Empress but the only result was an immediate order to quit the territory of the Empire; and on 12 January 1744 he was escorted to the frontier by a detachment of soldiers. And yet the Diaspora flourished in Livonia: a group of Livonian nobles, pastors and peasants continued to meet in the forests to share in the fellowship of the Lamb. Zinzendorf's witness had not been in vain. The day came when the Empress Catharine invited the Moravians to Moscow, and there they stayed until their Settlement was destroyed during the invasion of Napoleon in 1812.

The Moravians in Britain

The Moravians contributed mightily to the religious awakening in Great Britain. Indeed they were midwives to the Evangelical Revival and to the great Methodist movement. But again, under the inspiration of Zinzendorf, the motive was not to increase the Moravian Church, but simply to serve the cause of Christian unity

[1] *Sixteen Discourses on the Redemption of Man by the Death of Christ* (London, 1740).

124

by being 'a blessing and a salt in other religious denominations'.[1]

After the young Moravian, Peter Bohler, had preached in London, early in 1738, James Hutton (a London bookseller, the son of a High-Church clergyman and founder of two Religious Societies) wrote: 'This was something so very new to us all, so universal, so penetrating . . . (we had) tried to help ourselves; we dreamt not, we heard not, and knew not that our eternal welfare lay solely in Christ. Here therefore the evangelic period commenced in England.'[2] On 4 May 1738, John Wesley wrote in his *Journal*— 'Peter Bohler left London in order to embark for Carolina! Oh, what hath God begun, since his coming to England! Such an one as shall never come to an end till heaven and earth pass away.'[3] Before he sailed, Peter Böhler drew up a set of rules for the Religious Society at James Hutton's house, and for two years that Society was the very centre of the embryo Evangelical Revival. It was when the Moravians came with their heart-religion, glowing with the warmth of personal feeling; commending the Lamb by their fellowship and brotherly approach to all men and all denominations; letting men feel the love of Christ in their own self-denying, cheerful lives; appealing to the direct personal experience of the individual; and assuring their hearers that it was possible to know one's sins forgiven and to know Christ as a personal Saviour—it was then that the evangelical religion was set aflame again in England.

In 1728 Zinzendorf had sent three Brethren to London and Oxford. In 1735 Spangenberg had arranged in London the voyage of the 'first company' of Moravians to Georgia; the brave and serene behaviour of the Moravians on board the *Simmonds* during a great storm in the winter of 1736, first awakened Wesley to his own lack of a saving faith. In February 1737, Zinzendorf spent some time in London and established a Diaspora Society from among the attenders at the services in his household. No 5 of the rules he drew up for the Society shows clearly the intent of the members: 'We will not interfere in any religious or ecclesiastical matters, but

---

[1] C. W. Towlson, *Moravian and Methodist*, p. 169.
[2] D. Benham, *Memoirs of James Hutton*, p. 28. [3] Vol. i, pp. 457 f.

attend only to three simple things:—to become saved and sancti-fied by the blood of Jesus, and to love each other cordially.'

From February to May 1738 the Wesleys and Peter Bohler were in constant communion: travelling, praying and talking together. Methodist scholars have differed as to the exact interpretation of these conversations, but few have questioned their tremendous consequences.[1] They were immortal discourses. Peter Bohler brought dogma down from John Wesley's head and proved it along the pulses of his heart in the overwhelming joy of a personal experience and fellowship with Christ. It was probably William Holland, an Anglican member of Hutton's Religious Society and in union with the Moravians, who was the reader on that immortal evening of Wednesday 24 May 1738 when John Wesley entered into the Pentecostal experience to which the Moravian witness had been leading him: 'I went very unwillingly to a society in Alders-gate Street, where one was reading Luther's preface to the *Epistle to the Romans*. About a quarter before nine, while he was describing the change which God works in the heart through faith in Christ, I felt my heart strangely warmed. I felt I did trust in Christ, Christ alone for my salvation; and an assurance was given me that He had taken away my sins, even mine, and saved me from the law of sin and death.'[2] The Moravians had brought Wesley to that assurance and that theme which was to revolutionize the religion of his day and give birth to the thirteen million Methodists of our own times. 'It is true', he affirmed, 'that from May 24th 1738 wherever I was desired to preach, salvation by faith was my only theme.'[3]

It is interesting but futile to speculate on what might have been the course of English Church history if the Methodists and the Moravians had not finally separated after July 1740. The Moravian Church might have been the Methodist Church of today. But probably the separation was inevitable: differences of personality, principle and background made it so. For example, 'the great deal

---

[1] E.g. 'Methodism owes more . . . to Moravianism than to any other religious movement.' Henry Bett, *The Spirit of Methodism*, p. 50.
[2] *Journal*, vol. i, p. 476.   [3] *Letters*, vol. ii, p. 65.

of plain man' in John Wesley could not grasp the absolute insistence of the Moravians on the Divine initiative. As R. A. Knox wrote, 'there was a fine instinct about the Moravian distrust of "willing and shalling", the Moravian aspiration to replace the sense of duty by a sense of dynamic liberty;'[1] but for the Wesley of the 1740's these things were turned into mystic vapourings by the Moravian overstatement of them. Both Wesley and Zinzendorf tended to regard each other with suspicion as 'Pope' of their respective communions. But that the broad influence of Zinzendorf's ecumenical witness touched the heart of Wesley cannot be doubted. Zinzendorf would have welcomed wholeheartedly a passage in a letter from Wesley to his old Moravian friend, James Hutton, written on 26 December 1771: 'If we do not yet think alike, we may at least love alike.'[2]

In a very short time the Moravian Diaspora made a decisive impact in many parts of the British Isles. On 14 March 1740 James Hutton wrote to Zinzendorf, informing him that 'in Wales some thousands are stirred up . . . the young man Howell Harry (Howell Harris), who has been a great instrument in this work, is exceeding teachable and humble, and loves the Brethren'.[3] In response to a request made by a Scottish lord and member of Parliament in the name of a group of Presbyterian ministers, a Moravian student spent some weeks in Edinburgh in 1743 informing inquirers about the Brethren.[4] In addition to many Anglicans and Methodists, the Brethren also won the admiration of men like the Quaker, Thomas Erskine of Edinburgh; the famous Independent minister of Northampton, Philip Doddridge, who rejoiced in a letter of 1741 in 'the success of our dear Moravian Brethren and their associates';[5] and of representative men like David Hartley and John Byrom.[6]

In April 1741 Spangenberg was sent as 'General Helper' to organize and superintend the Moravian work in England. His calm wisdom brought unity into the Fetter Lane Society and in May 1741 he

[1] *Op. cit.*, p. 479. [2] *Letters*, vol. v, p. 294. [3] Benham, *op. cit.*, p. 48.
[4] Holmes, *op. cit.*, vol. ii, p. 42. [5] Benham, *op. cit.*, p. 59.
[6] Henri Tallon, *John Byrom* (London, 1950), p. 188.

focused the members' support for foreign missions in the Society for the Furtherance of the Gospel. There were at least eight branch Societies at Aldersgate Street, Islington, Wapping, Hampstead, Kensington, and at Little Moorfield.

But the Moravian Diaspora was spreading an evangelical revival beyond the bounds of London. Already in November 1739, the Moravian John Toeltschig had been invited by Benjamin Ingham, the Vicar of Osset, to help in carrying the gospel to the working folk in the area of Halifax, Leeds, Bingley and Wakefield. And again in response to an invitation from Ingham, the 'Pilgrim' congregation in Fetter Lane had set out for Yorkshire in May 1742 to establish a centre for the North. Under the leadership of Spangenberg these twenty-six Moravians set up their headquarters at Smith House in Lightcliffe, near Halifax, in July 1742. By the end of 1743 no less than forty-seven preaching-places had been established. In February 1743 Zinzendorf arrived in Yorkshire for talks with Ingham. By 1755 a Settlement on the full pattern of Herrnhut grew up at Fulneck, near Leeds, and in the same year Congregations were recognized at Lower Wyke, Mirfield and Gomersal. From these centres new points of contact were established in York, Swaledale and North Wales.[1]

Again it was the influence of the Moravians among the Anglican clergy which led to a religious awakening in Bedfordshire. In 1738 the smallpox raged so fearfully in Bedford that over sixty persons died in one week and many of the ministers of religion fled to safety. The Rev. Jacob Rogers, curate-in-charge of St Paul's Parish Church, remained at his post and sent for help to his old friend, Benjamin Ingham. Ingham brought with him William Delamotte who had also worked with the Moravians in Georgia and London. They lodged at the house of Francis Okely in the High Street. Okely also knew the Moravians well, having spent some years in Germany and translated Zinzendorf's sermons. Thus it was that Rogers was introduced to the Moravians who now came down from London and set many hearts on fire by their open-

---

[1] See *A History of Christianity in Yorkshire* (ed. F. S. Popham), ch. 8.

air preaching and conversations. Rogers, Delamotte and Okely became members of the Moravian Church and when James Hutton came down to Bedford he found 'many souls who were hearty in the Lord's cause'.[1] By 1742 there were groups of people working for a religious revival in twenty-one of the surrounding villages.

For the Moravian work in North Cheshire and South Lancashire a centre was established at Dukinfield, six miles from Manchester, in 1743. Toeltschig and other Moravians from Yorkshire initiated this work in response to an invitation from David Taylor, a friend of Benjamin Ingham. Toeltschig had already established a centre for the Moravian Diaspora in the Midlands at a delightful village called Ockbrook, near Derby in 1740.

In the West of England and in Ireland the Moravian witness was powerfully extended by the former Methodist evangelist, John Cennick.[2] The heart-religion, the fellowship and the joy of the Moravians had taken strong hold of Cennick by May 1742 when he wrote: 'I love brother Spangenberg dearly, my heart is with his heart in the Lord Jesus.'[3] Cennick was the first to introduce the Revival into Ireland, where it ran like wild-fire throughout County Antrim and expectant areas in the south. The speed of the success can be measured by the fact that within one year from June 1746 Cennick had established a Society in Dublin numbering 526: 89 married men, 117 married women, 87 single men and boys, 170 single women and 63 widows.

Only a Gazeteer would suffice to enumerate the Moravian preaching-places and Societies formed in the mid-eighteenth century.[4] The Moravian horsemen rode thousands of miles all over the British Isles preaching the gospel of the Cross and the unity of all men in the Lamb. But the Moravian Church herself in England did not grow. Never before perhaps in the history of Christian

[1] Benham, *op. cit.*, p. 103.
[2] See J. E. Hutton, *John Cennick* (London, 1906). Zinzendorf called Cennick 'Paul Revived'.
[3] J. E. Hutton, *John Cennick* (London, 1906), p. 31.
[4] See a series of sketches by John England of *The work carried on by the Ancient Protestant Episcopal Moravian Church* (pub. in Leeds and London, 1886–90).

expansion have so effective a band of witnesses ever made so determined and successful an effort to discourage the growth of their own church.

The Diaspora idea was dominant in England. And the character of the Diaspora was to gather not friends of the Moravian Church, but the true children of God in all the world. Zinzendorf did not wish to establish Moravian congregations in every place, but *Gemeine* of Jesus Christ. The Diaspora was to be a step along the ecumenical road and the means whereby the life and unity of the existing denominations could be restored. And Zinzendorf was never able to reconcile this conception with the establishment of a fully organized Moravian Church which, as we have seen, historical circumstances made inevitable. This unresolved tension between the Diaspora-idea and the Church-idea plagued Zinzendorf to the end, as it did most of the Moravian leaders throughout the eighteenth century.

'Since one of the Protestant religions is as dear to us as the other', the Moravians stated in an English Synod, 'therefore it is that we can never make it our business to gain proselytes either for one or the other, but we direct all souls to Jesus Christ, as the Head and Lord of His Church.'[1] Their complete unattachment to any 'sectarian way' was noted by James Erskine, High Steward of Scotland, in a letter to Zinzendorf 10 April 1742: 'We see the Brethren running unweariedly to gain souls for Christ, and minding nothing else.'[2] That the Moravians were not concerned with denominational expansion is clearly illustrated by the fact that after two years' work in Yorkshire, the Diaspora attached to the Moravian enterprise had 1,200 members—but the Congregation members of the Moravian Church in that area numbered only sixty-two.

The Moravians sought to rival no denomination: 'We avoid all ground or places', they declared, 'which other servants of God,

---

[1] Towlson, *Moravian and Methodist*, p. 169.

[2] John England, *Short Sketches of the work carried on by the Ancient Protestant Episcopal Moravian Church in Lancashire, Cheshire, The Midlands, and Scotland* (Leeds, 1888), p. 42.

with or without right, do dispute with us: from the maintenance of which, little blessings would ensue.'[1] In Sheffield, for example, despite the protests of their converts, the Moravians withdrew and gave place to the Methodists who had come to the town. Moreover, in England the Moravians only went where they had a clear invitation. It was only when Ingham's society members gave them a unanimous invitation that Spangenberg and the Pilgrim Congregation agreed to go to Yorkshire. Cennick tells how the Moravians were invited to take the leadership in the Wiltshire revival: 'On Monday 15 December, 1745, we had a conference with the stewards . . . they met again, and unanimously signed an invitation to the Brethren to come among them, proposing to give up themselves wholly to their care, giving them authority to alter, change or do whatever they should see fit among them, and the Societies under their care.'[2]

The Moravians were only too pleased when they could lead their Diaspora adherents back to the local parish church for the ministration of the vicar. An entry in the Moravian London Congregation *Diary* shows how careful they were to do nothing inimical to the good order of the Anglican Church: 'Our Society Brethren and Sisters must not expect to have their children baptised by us. It would be against all good order to baptise their children. The increase of this United Flock (Diaspora Society) is to be promoted by all proper means, that the members of it may be a good salt to the Church of England.'[3] The ideal conduct for the Diaspora members in all countries was laid down by Zinzendorf in a speech in June 1750: 'The Diaspora should especially not affect anything new or unaccustomed, but in all quietness conduct themselves according to their church organizations, and to be distinguished from their neighbours by nothing else than the quality of their spiritual life, so that everything the Brethren do proceeds from their hearts in their church life as well as in their life in society.'[4]

[1] *Acta Fratrum*, p. 82. [2] *Moravian Messenger*, vol. xi, p. 378.
[3] J. E. Hutton, *A History of the Moravian Church*, p. 445.
[4] See J. R. Weinlick, 'The Moravian Diaspora', *Transactions of the Moravian Historical Society* (Nazareth, Pa., 1959), vol. xvii, pt. i, p. 35.

Such an irenic and ecumenical policy of course kept the Moravian Church small in membership. And Zinzendorf wished it to be so. Only in very special cases were the members of the Diaspora Societies allowed to join the Moravian Church: if they had for many years ceased to take the Holy Communion in the parish church; if they felt a clear call from God to 'leave the world' and for their own inner peace or for the dedication of their lives to special service to enter a Moravian Settlement both as a refuge for their souls and as a training ground for service in the army of the Lamb. In short, they were only admitted into membership of the Moravian Church if 'they could in no otherwise come through the world'; and even then their admission had to be confirmed by the Lot.

It was Zinzendorf's conviction that it was only by forgetting any denominational ambition of their own that the Moravians could keep in fresh memory and effective practice their interdenominational witness and reconciliation. Where Moravian Settlements were established they were to be regarded as the 'Saviour's Armoury', citadels of training, where each member was to be committed to a definite task, governed under strict discipline, and to be at the immediate call of the Lamb for service in any part of the world. And this conception of the Moravian Settlements explains why their membership was fenced around with so many tests and inquiries. It was not that the Moravians regarded themselves as better than other Christians (although that misunderstanding inevitably arose in the minds of the outsiders) but simply that to be a Moravian meant acceptance of a rigorous and full obedience to a Christian discipline which brooked no denial. The convictions of a Moravian member had to be strong enough to bear the Cross of the Church. If a man did not have these uttermost convictions—good Christian as he may be—it was better for him to stay outside the Settlements and serve God in the Societies. Of course, as often in Christian history, practice lagged behind the ideal; mistakes were made; and the Moravians sometimes had to lament that 'many a one, who shines as a light in the Diaspora, is lamed when he comes among us, and is a burden to us'.

In the Diaspora and the Pilgrim Congregation the good news of the love of God was refreshed to the hearts of many tired Christians throughout Christendom and they laboured as children of peace in their own and other Churches. This perhaps above all was the service of the Diaspora—to be a child of peace: one Moravian, Konrad Lange, who began his 'pilgrim journey' in 1738, set down the matter succinctly for us: 'Where factions and parties are, there is one a child of peace. One does not align himself with any party, but one seeks to bring the various sentiments to the fundamentals, to the merits and death of Jesus, through which all sectarianism disappears by itself.'[1]

Family and Finance

Amidst all their labours and journeyings it was not possible for the Moravian 'messengers' to have a settled home life for long. But it was only what they expected. Zinzendorf had told them so and he gave them a bright example himself. In everything the 'work of the Lamb' must come first. Indeed, joined together in the service of the Lamb, the Moravian husband and wife could never be separated no matter what stretch of ocean or continent lay between them.[2]

A little before he married the Countess Erdmuth Dorothea von Reuss on 7 September 1722, Zinzendorf wrote to his grandmother: 'There will be some difficulties for I am but a poor match, and, I confess the Countess will have to content herself with a life of self-denial. She will have to cast all ideas of rank and quality to the winds, as I have done, for they are not things of divine institution but inventions of human vanity. If she wishes to aid me, she must give herself to what is the sole object of my life—namely, to win souls for Christ, and that in the midst of contempt and reproach.'[3] The Countess bravely met these demands all through her life. Born into a devout Pietist home at the castle of Ebersdorf, she was

---

[1] Weinlick, *op. cit.*, p. 31.

[2] When Rosalie Nitschmann was once asked in Herrnhut if she was anxious about her husband away in America, she replied: 'No! He is the Saviour's servant. But we are very fond of one another.'

[3] F. Bovet, *The Banished Count*, p. 65.

admirably fitted by training and by temperament to give her husband the kind of help that he needed, a help that touched his chosen vocation at every point. The Count and the Countess, wrote John Holmes, 'were one heart and soul, not only in their conjugal relation, but in their determination to consecrate themselves, their children, their time and their wealth to Christ and his service'.[1]

Although never strong in health, the Countess accompanied her husband on many of his journeys and voyages. Wherever their wanderings kept them together she made a home for him, and whenever she could not accompany him she still kept her house as a centre of the Moravian enterprise and as a haven for the many 'messengers' who arrived from all parts of the world. She knew little domestic comfort or privacy. Often, it was said, from six o'clock in the morning until eleven at night she was busy in the service of the brethren and sisters who came to her home. Only seldom did she retire for rest to her own little corner with its table and curtain, and not even then without an apology. She was constantly at work managing affairs, writing hymns, holding conferences, and exercising a spiritual ministry among the Sisters of the Pilgrim Congregation or the Settlement where she happened to be.

With their own great love for children it must have been no light trial for Zinzendorf and his wife to be separated so much from their own family; for like the Count, the Countess too was often away on business for the Diaspora, advising and mediating tactfully in the differences which arose with the civil and ecclesiastical authorities. The Countess bore twelve children, six sons and six daughters. Only four of them reached maturity and only three—Benigna, Mary Agnes and Elizabeth—outlived their parents. On more than one occasion, both the Count and his wife were away on their travels when their children died. The last surviving son, Christian Renatus, died at the age of twenty-four on 28 May 1752 in London and was buried in the Moravian ground at Chelsea.[2] The

[1] *History of the Protestant Church of the United Brethren*, vol. i, p. 419.
[2] See Wilhelm Jannasch, 'Christian Renatus Graf von Zinzendorf', *Zeitschrift für Brüdergeschichte* (Herrnhut), vol. ii (1908), pp. 45–68, vol. iii (1909), pp. 66–89.

Countess arrived too late from Herrnhut to see him alive. She had loved her son tenderly and she was deeply affected. Something of the lonely pathos which must have struggled in her heart more than once for expression comes out in a letter she wrote at this time: 'I must return with empty hand and leave behind my precious Christelein. O how deeply it cuts . . . I have been to Chelsea three times. Tears are not few while one is there. On no day have I been without them. To Papa I have had to put on a brave front.'[1] As a true Moravian, the Countess had learned to keep her sorrows stored up in her heart, but after the death of Christian Renatus, writes Spangenberg, she had no longer 'much inclination for occupying herself with outward affairs, but was like a weary pilgrim who longs for repose'.[2] In four years she was dead.

The Moravian Church in the eighteenth century owed much to the Countess. And not least were her gifts of good sense, sound judgment and wise administration. Without her careful oversight the Moravian Church might well have foundered in the early days.

Throughout Zinzendorf's lifetime there was a perpetual financial strain in the administration of the Moravian enterprise. The Count himself had little business acumen to match his dreams for the world mission. He certainly wanted nothing for himself. His dress was always simple and even careless; his house was never well furnished; and he was said to have been incorrigibly regardless of his own comfort. He gave himself and all that he had for the 'work of the Lamb' and he expected everyone else to do the same.[3] It was well that he immediately recognized the shrewd and methodical attributes of his wife and as soon as they were married he made over his estates to her—an arrangement which was legally ratified in

---

[1] Wilhelm Jannasch, *Erdmuth Dorothea Gräfin von Zinzendorf*, p. 480; quoted in J. R. Weinlick, *Count Zinzendorf*, p. 209. To the Moravians, Zinzendorf was 'Papa' and the Countess 'Mama'.

[2] *Zinzendorf*, p. 461.

[3] 'Our missions among the heathen have been furthered and supported with great zeal and concern of heart by the late Count Zinzendorf, from their very beginning to his entering into the joy of his Lord.' Benjamin La Trobe, *A Succinct View of the Missions established among the Heathen by the Church of the Brethren, or Unitas Fratrum* (London, 1771), p. 27.

1732. At least down to the death of Christian Renatus, the Countess remained as the 'economy' head of the Zinzendorf property and of the Pilgrim Congregation. And she, like her husband, squandered nothing on trifles or vain show; but, again like her husband, 'when the destitute were to be relieved, or the cause of God promoted, she distributed with a bountiful hand, and often beyond her ability'.[1]

But the burden of finance remained heavy and was to get worse. It is true that the Moravian ministers and missionaries received little in payment that they did not earn for themselves,[2] but the maintenance of the vast world liaison, the dispatch of colonists, the purchase or lease of land, the erection of Settlements and church buildings, the upkeep of the boarding schools and the parliamentary negotiations—all these made heavy demands on the Moravian purse.

Zinzendorf's attitude in these circumstances was seldom realistic. He was opposed in principle to collections. He was very willing to receive gifts—from the royal houses of Denmark and Holland, for example—and to negotiate loans for the work, but he disliked appeals for aid and the taking of regular contributions. 'When we are desired to make Establishments', he wrote, 'here and there, it is always at our own expence; and if loans are offered to us in order to facilitate the matter, we repay it with all speed.'[3] When he was made aware of distress, he quickly came to the rescue. He immediately gave a personal security for £10,000 when the financial crisis among the Moravians in England came to a head in 1753.[4]

At Zinzendorf's death in 1760, his own estates, which he had promised to the Brethren to support their finances, were left heavily

---

[1] John Holmes, *op. cit.*, vol. i, p. 418.

[2] On some mission fields, as in Labrador, it was not easy for the missionaries to support themselves: 'thus the Brethren must be supported chiefly by the provision sent to them annually from Europe, such as flour, salt meat, rice, peas and barley.' *A Brief Account of the Mission established among the Esquimaux Indians on the coast of Labrador* (London, 1774, anon. La Trobe probably), p. 29.

[3] *An Exposition, op. cit.*, pt. ii, p. 48.

[4] See D. Benham, *Memoirs of James Hutton*, pp. 265—80.

mortgaged; and there was a debt of £150,000. But the Moravians girded themselves: they bought the estates of Berthelsdorf and Gross-Hennersdorf from Zinzendorf's daughters for £25,000; they settled a pension for life on Benigna, Mary Agnes and Elizabeth; and they took over the whole debt. By 1801 only £10,800 of the initial debt remained and this was assumed by the firm of Abraham Durninger and Co, in Herrnhut.

8

A CONGREGATION OF GOD
IN THE SPIRIT

―――――――

The Plan for Unity

ZINZENDORF longed to see the invisible or true Church of
Christ made visible on earth. It was always a great joy to see
the 'christed souls' of the different denominations gathered together
in the name of the Lamb and sharing 'any experience of what grace
our Saviour is'. 'This is a blessed concourse', the Count wrote, 'to
see such a multitude of souls enamoured with our Saviour in one
meeting, and a number of guests together, who will sup with one
another, and together salute the holy wounds.'[1] But he felt that
something more was needed than the visible unity shed abroad in
the structure and labours of the Diaspora. 'Father,' he prayed, 'let
things be brought so far in the world, that a Church be seen, that
a People may be seen, which acts in Thy name, and appeals to the
Marriage-Supper of the Father of Jesus Christ, which He makes
for His Son, the King.'[2] As we have said, Zinzendorf's search for the
visible unity of all Christians did not embrace the organic union
of all the different Churches in a single Church with one order and
one discipline: he envisaged the fulfilment of what Archbishop
Lord Fisher referred to in his sermon at Rome in 1960 as 'the ancient
and apostolic conception of a Commonwealth of Churches within
one Church of Christ'.

Zinzendorf's own title for this commonwealth of Churches
within one Church of Christ was a Congregation of God in the

―――――――

[1] Fetter Lane *Discourses*, p. 56.   [2] *Ibid.*, p. 27.

138

Spirit, and first we must notice that, as in all things, Jesus Christ was to be recognized as the Head of this Congregation. The recognition of the Headship of Christ in all Moravian affairs is associated with the events of 16 September 1741. On that day a conference of Moravian leaders including Zinzendorf and Spangenberg, at a house in Red Lion Street, London, met to discuss the resignation of Leonard Dober from the office of Chief Elder. It came upon them that Jesus Christ alone is the Chief Elder, the Bishop of souls and the Head of the Church. 'We promise on our part', wrote the Brethren, 'that we would love and honour Him as our Elder, and through His grace keep up an uninterrupted and confidential heart's intercourse with Him; that we would childlikely obey His will and direction, choosing no man as our head in spiritual matters, but cleave to Him with full purpose of heart, though all others should forsake Him.' On that day the long known Headship of Christ was transformed from a theological formula into a fact of experience. The Moravian Church became a free Church in every sense. No absolute writ of any human authority was to run within her borders; the Brethren would bow to the will and law of Christ alone; and it was this conception of the Headship of Christ that Zinzendorf sought to realize in the Congregation of God in the Spirit.

It was particularly in the vital decade of the 1740's that Zinzendorf tried to make clear to himself and to his generation *Die Tropenidee*, or the Tropus idea, by which the Congregation of God in the Spirit might be brought into being.

The Tropus idea or plan (from the Greek *tropoi peideias*—methods of training) was based on Zinzendorf's recognition of the manifoldness of life and revelation. Each of the Churches (Denominations) of Christendom was a Tropus, 'a school of wisdom', with its own particular 'Jewel' of truth, ritual or order, to contribute to whole Body of Christ in setting forth the full glory and mission of the Lamb. In each Tropus—the Lutheran, Calvinist, Anglican, Moravian, Mennonite, for example, and indeed in the ultramontane Roman Catholic and the Gallican—the Lamb was preparing his 'christed ones' for their membership in the one Universal

Church. Zinzendorf would have none of these Tropuses destroyed, although none of them was an end in itself. 'If thou wilt follow the example of Jesus, thou must not be so very forward to conceive scruples against thy own Religion (i.e. Church, Denomination, Tropus). All the truths held forth to thee there, and which approve themselves as such to thy heart, embrace gladly; yet still maintain thy respect and affection for the constitution itself.'[1] 'Religions (Tropuses) are God's economy, machinery to bring Truth and the Love of His Son to men according to their capacity, and according to the temperature and atmosphere of the country. For England the English Religion is suitable; in the Spanish and Portuguese atmosphere, the Catholic; for the French temperament the last is not quite so fitting; hence the Gallican Church, a *misch-masch* of Catholic and Reformed with more Freedom than in other Catholic countries. Protestantism suits Germany and still more the northern lands. The Saviour has all the Religions (Tropuses) under His protection and will not let them be destroyed.'[2]

How then, Zinzendorf asked, could the 'christed ones' of the different Tropuses be brought together in some firmer field of encounter than the Diaspora? How could they meet in some ecumenical structure, still keeping and quickening their particular Denominational treasure, and yet learning from each other in mutual discovery, rendering a common witness in a common calling, seeking afresh the full dimensions of the Universal Church, and rediscovering that unity which they already shared in the Lamb of God, the Head of the Church? Was there anywhere a valid Christian communion of irenic and ecumenical traditions, a servant to all the Churches, seeking no dominion herself, careless of her own life and growth, which could provide a resting-place, a place of union, an inn for the members of the Invisible Church made visible? Yes, there was the ancient Unitas Fratrum, now renewed in the Moravian Church and prepared through long years of trial and illumination for this very purpose. She could form that

---

[1] *Maxims*, p. 333.
[2] O. Uttendörfer, *Zinzendorfs Weltbetrachtung* (Berlin, 1929), p. 79.

comprehensive ark to shelter and gather together members from every Tropus under heaven.[1]

As Knox put it, Zinzendorf meant the Moravian Church 'to be a kind of religious order within the framework of Protestant Christendom, acting as a liaison between the rival sects by confusing its own outlines, and remaining always on terms with the religion of the country. Lutheranism in Germany, Anglicanism in England, should be united in spite of themselves because each had a concordat with Moravianism.'[2] Zinzendorf himself splendidly said: "'Tis not properly our business to enlarge the knowledge of Christians of whatever Denomination, or to correct their principles; but to refresh to them the Image of Jesus, the tormented form of our suffering God, which in all those Denominations is acknowledged, and esteemed reverend.'[3] The Unitas Fratrum was the mother of all the Protestant Churches and such were her order and faith that all the 'christed ones' could feel at home within her borders. 'I may compare them', Lord Granville said in a speech supporting the *Acta Fratrum* of 1749, 'to a casting-net over all Christendom, to enclose all denominations of Christians. If you like episcopacy, they have it; if you choose the Presbytery of Luther or Calvin, they have that also; and if you are pleased with Quakerism, they have something of that.'[4]

The Moravian Church was indeed richly blessed for her ecumenical office as hostess to the Tropuses, and when her purpose was accomplished she could vanish from the scene. 'For the present', Zinzendorf said, 'the Saviour is manifesting His *Gemeine* to the world in the outward form of the Moravian Church; but in fifty years that Church will be forgotten.'[5] Indeed when each Tropus has learnt the lesson of unity within the Congregation of God in the Spirit, then that Tropus too will pass away, and the ecumenical reign will be brought nearer.

The Pennsylvanian Experiment

From the letters of 1736–9 sent to him by Spangenberg,

[1] *Maxims*, p. 357; Hutton, *op. cit.*, p. 273. [2] *Enthusiasm*, p. 419.
[3] *Maxims*, p. 93. [4] Hutton, *op. cit.*, p. 345. [5] Hutton, *op. cit.*, p. 262.

Zinzendorf concluded that Pennsylvania was the very place where an evangelical commonwealth of the Churches in a Congregation of God in the Spirit might be realized. No State or Established Church existed there to accuse him of schism. There was a clamant need of unity; there was ample opportunity for an ecumenical co-operation in evangelism and education among the settlers and the Indians; and the Moravians, although not organized there, had some footing in the land.

In 1740 Pennsylvania was bounded on the west by the Susquehanna river, and on the north by the Blue Mountains. Within it were large areas of primeval forest and beyond it lay the wilderness. The religious liberty which so many of the German settlers had come to enjoy in Pennsylvania had degenerated into a religious anarchy. Churches and sects abounded—mostly intent on their own way and resentful of the independence of others: there were Lutherans, Calvinists or Reformed (of divers confessions), Episcopalians, Presbyterians, Independents, Separatists, Baptists, Quakers, Sabbatarians or Seventh-Day men, Unitarians, Schwenkfelders, Dunkers, Mennonites, French Prophets, Hermits, Newborn Ones, New-lights, Protestant Monks and Nuns and Free-thinkers. There were 100,000 Germans in Pennsylvania to whose spiritual needs there were not more than twelve regularly ordained men to minister. Worship, the rites and sacraments were neglected; thousands had never been baptized; and schools were as scarce as organized congregations. Those who yearned for some religious consolation were at a loss what to believe amidst the general confusion. Indeed it was a common saying that to belong to the 'Pennsylvania Church' was equivalent to being an infidel.

But, as Spangenberg wrote to Zinzendorf, 'one may indeed see signs of waking up here and there'. He told the Count of a group of men of different Denominations led by Henry Antes, a Reformed lay preacher, who from 1736 had met monthly as the 'Associated Brethren of Skippack' to plan a joint attack upon the prevailing religious disorder and ignorance. In 1739 Zinzendorf commissioned Andrew Eschenbach with other Moravians to travel through Pennsylvania, and by preaching and conversation to endeavour to unite those of all parties who appeared to love the Lord Jesus in sincerity. On 29 November 1741, together with his sixteen year old daughter Benigna and six other 'pilgrims', Zinzendorf himself landed in New York.

In preparation for his Pennsylvanian labours, Zinzendorf had reaffirmed the ecumenical purpose of his life and mission. 'I cannot with my testimony confine myself to one Denomination', he told the Moravians in conference at Herrendyk in August 1741, 'for the whole earth is the Lord's, and all souls are His; I am debtor to all.' That his undenominational purposes might be unhampered by narrower obligations and that he might be regarded in Pennsylvania as a free servant of the Church Universal, he had resigned his Moravian episcopate in the previous July. And now that his titles might not hinder his labours in the New World, the Count Zinzendorf announced to the Governor in Philadelphia, on 10 December 1741, that he wished to be known as Herr von Thurnstein.[1] On 20 December Zinzendorf met Henry Antes and inspired him (although the Skippack Association had ceased to meet) to send out a circular letter inviting representatives of all the denominations and sects to gather in conference at Germantown on 12 January 1742. Each 'beloved friend and brother' was invited 'not to dispute and wrangle, but converse in love on the essential articles of faith in order to discover how nearly all true Christians approximate in the fundamentals of religion; to come to a mutual agreement respecting all such opinions as do not affect the ground of salvation, and to bear with each other in love, that thus all uncharitable judging might be lessened and moved out of the way'.[2]

The immediate outcome of Antes' letter was the inauguration of the famous Pennsylvania Synods which continued to meet until 1748. Our chief concern here is with the seven Synods which met

[1] Thurnstein was one of his family names. He was also called Brother Ludwig and Johanan. The Quakers called him Friend Louis. But everyone knew him to be and treated him as the Count von Zinzendorf.

[2] John Holmes, *History of the Protestant Church of the United Brethren* (London, 1825), vol. i, p. 371.

between January and June 1742 and in which—as was to be expected—Zinzendorf took the leading part. The average attendance at the Synods was over a hundred delegates and visitors from nearly all the 'religions' in Pennsylvania. There were Lutherans, Reformed, Mennonites, Schwenkfelders, Baptists, Dunkers, Separatists, Hermits and Moravians. The Episcopalians, Presbyterians and Quakers held a watching brief.

The first Synod was held at Germantown, 12–13 January 1742. Zinzendorf was invited to speak and he soon made known his chief intent. 'I wished to make use of this opportunity', he wrote afterwards, 'to place on the throne the Lamb of God as the real Creator, Preserver, Redeemer and Sanctifier of the whole world, and at the same time to introduce in *theoria et praxis* the catholicity of the doctrine of His Passion as a universal theology for the German Pennsylvanians.'[1] Founded on this resolve his grand purpose was to unite all the Denominations in a Congregation of God in the Spirit. There was to be an interchange of ministers, intercommunion, and a widespread alliance in the work of evangelism and education. But denominational membership was still to be retained, and it is interesting to note that, in accordance with the Tropus idea, the Moravians were registered at the Synods according to the Church in which they had been nurtured as children: Zinzendorf, Christopher Pyrlaeus and Laurence Nyberg were registered as Lutherans. When, on the second day of the Synod, the Separatists objected to any close connection between the denominations, they were answered in a truly Zinzendorfian statement. The true Church, or communion of saints, it was declared, 'is the Congregation of God in the Spirit throughout the whole world, constituting that spiritual body whose Head is Christ. But they also constitute a communion of saints who, though outwardly belonging to different Denominations, agree in all essential points of doctrine pertaining to salvation.'

At the second Synod held in Falkner Swamp, 25–26 January, Zinzendorf was elected President and once again he inspired the

---

[1] L. T. Reichel, *The Early History of the Church of the United Brethren in North America, 1734–48* (Nazareth, Pa., 1888), p. 99.

main resolution. 'The proper object of this assembly of all evan-gelical Denominations is, that henceforth a poor inquirer for the way of life may not be directed in twelve different ways, but only in one, let him ask whom he will. But if any one should take fancy to him who directed him in the way, and should wish to travel on the same according to his method, he has full liberty to do so, provided he be as yet in no connection with any religious society.'

The third Synod held in John de Turck's house at Oley, 21–23 February, witnessed events which, set in the ecclesiastical climate of their day, must always rank amongst the most remarkable and inspiring in the whole ecumenical story. Through the labours of the Moravian lay preacher, Andrew Eschenbach, a small band of Christians including Lutherans, Reformed and Mennonites had been gathered together at Oley; and now they were ready for formal recognition as a Moravian Congregation. But Zinzendorf would have none of this; it was not the purpose of the Moravians to proselytize, he argued; and he persuaded the Synod to establish the Oley Congregation as a non-denominational church with its members listed according to the Tropus or denomination in which they had been nurtured. Eschenbach was to be the minister and he was ordained together with two Moravian missionaries to the Indians, Christian Henry Rauch and Gottlob Buttner, and a Moravian who was minister-elect of the Lutheran church in Phila-delphia. The ordination was carried out, at the request of the Synod, by the Moravian bishop David Nitschmann, by Anthony Seiffert, a Moravian minister, and by 'Brother Ludwig as a theolo-gian from Tubingen'.[1] Following the ordinations, preparation was made for the baptism of three converted Indians, brought by Rauch from the Moravian station at Shekomeko. For nearly twelve hours on the day preceding the baptism, the three converts sat down with their fellow-Indians who had flocked to Oley at the news of the service and told them of the Lamb who had died for them. At the baptism, Shabash, Seim and Kiop were given the names of Abraham, Isaac and Jacob in the fond hope that they

---

[1] During his time in Pennsylvania, Zinzendorf regarded himself as a Lutheran minister (Pastor Thurnstein).

might prove to be the Patriarchs of the Christian Indian tribes.

Amidst these events, the whole Synod felt itself to be indeed a Congregation of God in the Spirit. Zinzendorf sent out letters to other Christian groups inviting them to come together. Plans were made for evangelism, for churches and schools, and for the provision of devotional literature. It was agreed that three Trustees, appointed by the Lot, should appoint two 'worthy children of God' to preserve the unity of the Congregation and to prevent it from deteriorating into just another Sect. In the diversity of the denominations, the Congregation would give a manifold praise and service to the one Lord and Saviour who joined them into one spirit.

Zinzendorf thought that here in Pennsylvania another Consensus of Sendomir had been achieved. But alas for the fragile hopes of man! After the third Synod the Congregation of God in the Spirit began to fall away. At the fifth Synod held in Germantown on 18–20 April only the Lutherans, Reformed and Moravians attended. A Moravian 'Sea Congregation', led by Peter Bohler, arrived in time to attend the seventh Synod at Philadelphia on 13–14 June. They were welcomed by Henry Antes who declared 'that the undenominational Synod of Pennsylvania acknowledges the old Moravian Church just arrived, as a true Church of the Lord'. Ninety-four of the members of this Synod were Moravians, and although quarterly Conferences were held until 1748, the representatives of the other denominations did not increase. The Pennsylvania Synods had virtually become Moravian Synods and, in recognition of this fact, Bishop John de Watteville (on an official visitation from Europe) formally organized the Moravian Church as a distinctive denomination in North America at a Synod held in Bethlehem, 12–16 October 1748.

There is often a paradox implicit in the growth of an ecumenical consciousness: it also encourages a denominational awareness, not always of an irenic nature. This happened in the Pennsylvania Synods. The controversy seems to have centred around the character and purpose of Zinzendorf. The sectarians could not forget his grand title nor his distinguished bearing; the European controversies were brought over to Philadelphia by the republication there of the anti-Moravian *Pastoral Letter* first issued in Amsterdam; the extreme Calvinists hated his rejection of the doctrine of reprobation; the Separatists hated his emphasis on the Church; and the Lutherans resented his alleged attempts to dictate their deliberations. Nothing was too mean to besmirch Zinzendorf's good name: the rumour was spread that Benigna was not his child but the offspring of some naval officer. One Sunday evening when the Count and his daughter were 'caught' writing hymns, a justice of the peace ordered them to desist, and on the next day they were fined eighteen shillings for profaning the sabbath.

Certainly at that time Zinzendorf's conception was not too clear, but many of the sectarians had no wish to understand it. His purpose seemed to them to be simply to enlarge the borders of the Moravian Church. But nothing could have been further from his mind. At Oley, as we have seen, he expressly forbade the formation of a Moravian congregation. The community of Moravians at Bethlehem (named by Zinzendorf on Sunday 24 December 1741) was first conceived by him as a centre for the Congregation of God in the Spirit. He would not countenance any proselytizing by the Moravian evangelists or the 'Pennsylvania Wagon' as they were sometimes called. It was only on condition that everything was done according to Lutheran practice that he allowed the Moravians to undertake the spiritual supervision of a group of Christians in the Maguntschi region in 1742. In May 1742 he accepted a call to become the pastor of the Lutherans in Philadelphia, and he built a new church for them on Race Street at his own expense; but he often preached for the Reformed Church in Germantown, and he planned to bring ministers from Europe for the congregations of this tradition. To accommodate the conscience of the Seventh-Day Baptists, he even set Saturday apart as a day of rest and prayer. Indeed, Zinzendorf did all to make clear that the Moravians, resting in Christ Crucified, were prepared to be all things to all men so that Christian unity might be served. There was certainly to be no Moravian denominational advance commensurate with the growing reach of Moravian influence: as in Europe, so in America, the function of the Moravian Church was to be a leaven of zeal and service and liaison among the other Churches.[1]

But Zinzendorf's ecumenical labours were not all in vain. The denominations were awakened to their responsibilities and to new life: Henry Melchior came from Europe to organize the Lutherans; and Michael Schlatter did the same for the Reformed Church in Pennsylvania. Among the schools which the Synods inspired was the first boarding school for girls in America: it was started by the Countess Benigna at Germantown in May 1742 and it developed into the Moravian Seminary and College for Women. With a fine creative drive and persistence, Zinzendorf produced devotional literature for all the Denominations who shared in the same famine of such material. During the two month voyage to America he had written hymns and theological essays. In Pennsylvania he compiled a Catechism, based on the results of the 1532 Synod of Berne, for the teachers of the Reformed Church in Germantown; and he published a volume called *Pastoral Hymns of Bethlehem*.

But perhaps the most tangible ecumenical result of the Pennsylvania Synods was the co-operation which followed in the mission to the Indians. At the very first Synod, Henry Antes had called upon the representatives of the churches to support the undenominational Moravian work for 'the furtherance of the Gospel' in North and South America and in the West Indies. Bands

---

[1] By 1749, under the brilliant leadership of Spangenberg, the Moravians had established thirty-two industries and farms in their 'Economy' at Bethlehem. They maintained fifty itinerant evangelists; they carried the gospel to the Indians; they organized Congregations in thirty-one localities in seven of the original American colonies; they established fifteen schools; they covered the costs of missionaries on their way to the West Indies and Surinam; and they were able to send funds to Europe to stabilize the Moravian finances there. But still in 1776 there were only nineteen Congregations in the Northern Province of the American Moravian Church. In 1779, a resolution was passed at Bethlehem, under the guidance of Bishop Reichel from Herrnhut, to the effect that 'in no sense shall the Societies of awakened, affiliated as the fruit of the former extensive itinerations, be regarded as preparatory to the organization of Congregations, and that membership in these Societies does not carry with it communicant membership or preparation for it'. It was not until 1857 that the American Moravians obtained their independence of the German benevolent despotism and moved into an era of denominational development.

of contributors were organized in Philadelphia and New York and in the homes of many of the synod members.

The vision and vigour of Zinzendorf laid hold upon the Indian mission. Caring nothing for his personal comfort (for ten days he lived entirely upon boiled beans) or safety, he made three journeys of exploration among the Indians in 1742. His main aim was to put the Indian mission upon a firm foundation by winning the friendship of the Six Nations of the powerful Iroquois Confederacy. On 24 July he set out from Bethlehem on horseback for the Indian village of Meniologameka, north of the Blue Mountains, and from thence he travelled to the home of Conrad Weiser, the official agent and interpreter for the Province of Pennsylvania, at Tulpehocken in Berks County. And there with three companions he was fortunate to meet eight deputies of the Six Nations who were returning from a meeting with Governor Thomas in Philadelphia. The deputies were proud men and not least the Chief Canassatego from Onodaga. It was a strange and critical meeting, but all was solved by the affection of a little Indian girl who ran up to Zinzendorf and kissed him as soon as he entered the room. She was the daughter of the Indian sagamore, named Caxhayton, who with his wife and child had been the welcome guests of Zinzendorf earlier in the year at Philadelphia. The Count asked that the Moravian missionaries might be granted freedom of movement and speaking among the Iroquois; and Canassatego agreed to this request confirming it by the present of a fathom of wampum of 186 white beads.

Later in August 1742 Zinzendorf visited Rauch's mission at Shekomeko and organized it into the first Indian Congregation of the Moravians in North America. Between 21 September and 9 November he travelled into the Wyoming valley of the upper Susquehanna and sealed a bond of friendship with Skikellimy, Chief of the Oneidas, at Shamokin. He moved on to the plains of the Shawnees whose reputation for treachery had not been exaggerated. They regarded Zinzendorf as a liar and a thief, intent upon exploiting the silver deposits in their lands. Three times he narrowly escaped death: once from scalping, once from poisoning by puff adders, and a third time from drowning when the girth of

149

his saddle broke and he was thrown from his horse into a creek. None of these perils were accidental. No wonder he reported that the Shawnees are 'a people wholly ignorant and averse to Christians and Christianity'. But before Zinzendorf left America in January 1743, he had planned the future of the Indian mission by the appointment of a General Manager and the nomination of twenty labourers to continue the work.

When in November 1745 Bishop Spangenberg organized the first American Missionary Society, called The Society for the Furtherance of the Gospel, many of the regular contributors and members were recruited from the Pennsylvania synodals: Henry Antes, Conrad Weiser and prominent men in various parts of Pennsylvania and New Jersey belonging to the Episcopalian, Lutheran and Reformed Churches. It was all very practical. As the Society Journal records, 'Michael Schaeffer declared that he would be at the service of the cause with his farm. Abraham Muller also pledged us his right hand to the undertaking.'

All in all, it may be said, that the Pennsylvania Synods failed in their chief purpose of unity because Zinzendorf was ahead of his time. As Dr Yoder has written, 'he dared to attempt what the boldest ecumenical minds of the nineteenth century only ventured to pen'.[1] But it is certain that the cause of Christian unity had been tackled as a vital issue and that many minds in the Pennsylvanian churches had been impressed with its vast importance.

Attempts in England

When Zinzendorf arrived back in Germany in 1743 he objected strongly to the steps which had been taken, in his absence, to increase the growth and recognition of the Moravian Church as a distinctive denomination. He regarded the Royal Letter of Frederick the Great, 25 December 1742, affirming that 'the Moravian Church under the government of her bishops shall be independent of the state church consistories' as quite out of keeping with his own conception of a non-sectarian fellowship which he had

---

[1] *A History of the Ecumenical Movement*, p. 230.

fostered since 1727. Zinzendorf could not annul the Royal Letter but at the Synod of Hirschberg, 1–12 July 1743, he so dominated the deliberations that in the following November he was invited to accept the title of *Advocatus et Ordinarius Fratrum* with full powers over the affairs of the Church.

It was a benevolent but firm despotism that Zinzendorf exercised. At the Synods of Marienborn in 1744 and 1745 he expounded his Tropus idea to the mystified acceptance of his hearers. The broad comprehensive Church—the 'tent' of the invisible Church of Christ—was to be known as the 'Church of the Brethren': it was to be a Unity of Brethren composed of every possible Tropus whose bond of unity is their fellowship in the Lamb—the 'unity of His wounds'. At the Synod of Lindheim, 12–27 July 1745, Zinzendorf declared that 'In future we will call ourselves simply Brethren, and our bishops, bishops of the Brethren. For to the Brethren's Church belong not only the Moravian Church but that made up of those Lutherans and Reformed who no longer exist in their own denominations because of their brutal theologians. We make use again of the right that rests upon the fact that formerly in Prague and in Poland there existed a Reformed and a Lutheran Moravian Church, which preserved their mutual creeds. Therefore we must now again use these terms in their general meaning.'[1] This Synod adopted boldly all the ecclesiastical offices which had been current in the Ancient Unity, as bishops, co-bishops, presbyters, deacons and acolytes; and they were to be regarded not merely as servants of the Moravian Church, but of the wider 'Church of the Brethren'.

Each Tropus within the 'Church of the Brethren' was to be led by a bishop (or later by 'administrators') of its own, who would also represent the Church beyond its borders. Polycarpus Muller was at the head of the Moravian Tropus; Frederick von Watteville at the head of the Reformed Tropus; and after George John Conradi, the General Superintendent of the Lutheran Church in

---

[1] See K. G. Hamilton, 'The Office of the Bishop in the Renewed Moravian Church' in *Transactions of the Moravian Historical Society* (Nazareth, Pa., 1954), vol. xvi, pt. i, p. 44.

Schleswig-Holstein, had declined on the grounds of age, Zinzendorf stood at the head of the Lutheran Tropus. Here at last, thought Zinzendorf, was the instrument required to gather in one all the 'christed ones' of God whilst yet preserving the heritage of all the denominations.

In September 1746 Zinzendorf came over to London and summoned a Synod to clarify the relationship between the Moravians and the Church of England and to consider the formation of an Anglican Tropus. As we have seen, the long acquaintance between the Unitas Fratrum and the Anglican Church had been vitally increased in the early days of the Evangelical Revival. Earlier in the century Daniel Ernst Jablonski had shared in a long correspondence with Archbishop Wake and other Anglican leaders in an attempt to unite the Unitas Fratrum with the Church of England on the basis of the episcopacy and the Book of Common Prayer.[1] Jablonski lamented the discarding of episcopacy by some Protestant churches on the Continent, and he rejoiced that the Unitas Fratrum had so carefully preserved it. He wrote to Patrick Gordon, one of his Anglican correspondents: 'Most assuredly I, the son, nephew, and great-nephew of a bishop who was born into the Unity of the Brethren (i.e., into that Church which, alone of the Churches beyond the seas, has preserved religiously in uninterrupted succession to this day the Episcopal Order which it received from the legitimate bishops in the age of Huss), and who have been nurtured in the Church of England, which almost alone so departed from the Church of Rome as not to depart from the Universal Church; I, as I affirm, cannot patiently bear the elimination from the Church of that most sacred Order, sacrosanct in the Church Universal from the apostolic age, and, if rightly established, by far the most useful to the Church.'[2] To a letter of 22 March 1717 in which Jablonski argued the validity of the episcopal succession of the Unitas Fratrum, Archbishop Wake replied: 'You have clearly demonstrated in your short treatise the episcopal succession in the Bohemian Churches; which for myself I had held to have been suffi-

---

[1] See pp. 128 f. *supra*.
[2] Norman Sykes, *Daniel Ernst Jablonski and the Church of England*, p. 1.

ciently proved by earlier writers'.[1] Although so much ecumenical correspondence did not result in the union which Jablonski desired, it did much to provide that climate of opinion in which Zinzendorf's claims on behalf of the Unitas Fratrum could be taken seriously and indeed lead to the recognition by the Parliament of Great Britain of the Unitas Fratrum as 'an ancient Protestant Episcopal Church'.

Zinzendorf deeply appreciated the wide tolerance and comprehensiveness of the Church of England and he longed for a closer unity between that communion and the Unitas Fratrum. In a letter of 22 August 1744 he reminded Edmund Gibson, Bishop of London, that the 'Moravian Brethren might, and ought to share with the English, the duty of preaching the gospel among the heathen, since they are orthodox, apostolic and episcopalian; and because of the proximity of their ritual with that of the Anglican Church'.[2] Again Bishop Gibson was informed that 'the Moravian Church and the English Church are not two different Churches, but two branches of the same Church'. The Moravian Brethren sought only to be the allies of the Anglicans in binding 'pious minds to the ancient altars, to bring back such as have been drawn away'; and to keep those 'within the fence' who might otherwise have been lost in 'the trackless wilds of Methodism' or 'the devious paths of the multifarious sects into which England is so surprisingly divided'. The Moravians sought no denominational increase or advantage in England: indeed, their constant advice to all who would join their membership is 'abide in the Church of England'; but when such conservatism is no longer practicable, Zinzendorf argued, 'it is certainly better that those moved by maternal affection towards children, should permit them to be assigned to the friendly care of the Moravian Brethren, rather than that, wrested from their charge, they should be permitted to fall, or be precipitated into the bosom of the sects less orthodox, less regularly constituted, and less friendly to the Anglican Church'. At all times, Zinzendorf had a most tender care for the unity of the Church of England and

[1] Norman Sykes, *William Wake* (Cambridge, 1957), vol. ii, p. 8.
[2] Daniel Benham, *Memoirs of James Hutton*, p. 158.

he would not willingly countenance any action to threaten that unity. As further proof of the ecumenical purpose of the Moravians, Zinzendorf introduced the bishop to the Tropus idea. 'The Moravian church-guardians are such practical philophers', he wrote, 'as entirely refuse receiving among them any member of another Protestant religion (Denomination); having made it a fundamental rule in one of their Synods that Calvinist, Lutheran, and strict Moravian members are to be governed by such Moravian bishops as originally derive from their respective confessions.'[1] On 2 August 1745 the *Daily Advertiser* published a 'Declaration' by Zinzendorf in which the desire for an Anglican Tropus was revealed: 'We wish for nothing more than that some time or other there might be some Bishop or parish minister found of the English Church, to whom, with convenience, and to the good liking of all sides, we could deliver the care of those persons of the English Church who have given themselves to our care.'[2]

In furtherance of his plan for an Anglican Tropus, Zinzendorf persuaded the London Synod of 1746 to agree to the use, among the English Moravians, of the Book of Common Prayer; to the joint-ordination of Moravian ministers by Anglican and Moravian bishops; and to the appointment in due time of a bishop as superintendent of the Anglican Tropus—an office which the Count himself would hold in the meantime. That same month, Zinzendorf dispatched letters to Dr Potter, Archbishop of Canterbury, outlining the plan for the Anglican Tropus. He makes it as clear as he can that it was never his intention to 'bring the English Church to the Moravian constitution, but the Moravian Church which dwells in England, in America, and the English people which have given themselves over to them out of all sorts of constitutions, to the plain English constitution'.[3] The Archbishop is reminded that Zinzendorf had always objected to the Fetter Lane Congregation calling itself 'The Brethren in Union with the Moravian Church', and had welcomed the Archbishop of York's suggestion that they

---

[1] Benham, *op. cit.*, pp. 158–67. [2] *Ibid.*, p. 182.
[3] The letters are given in Appendix C of Addison's *The Renewed Church of the United Brethren*, p. 183.

should 'stile themselves Brethren in Union with the English Church'.[1] The Count requested Dr Potter 'that your Grace might be pleased to take on yourself the Burden of the first Episcopal Administration' of the Anglican Tropus.[2] The Archbishop received the letters and Zinzendorf's messengers most graciously, but he could not accept the office, nor could he sanction the use of the Anglican Liturgy outside the Established churches. Archbishop Potter died in 1747 and official consideration of the Anglican Tropus ceased for the time being.

When the British Parliament recognized the Unitas Fratrum as 'an ancient Protestant Episcopal Church', with the approval of the Anglican bishops and of the sixteen Presbyterian lords,[3] Zinzendorf's objection to the Moravians being classed as Dissenters was met—in theory at least; but in practice their churches continued to be licensed as 'places of worship for the use of Protestant Dissenters'. It cannot be emphasized too much that, according to Zinzendorf, it was not the 'Moravian Brethren' who were recognized by the *Acta Fratrum* of 1749, but that broad and comprehensive Unity of Brethren, the 'tent' of the Tropuses, whose unity was in the Lamb slain for all men. Indeed Zinzendorf announced that he was prepared to lose the Act of Recognition rather than countenance the name 'Moravian Brethren' which seemed to him to imply a church organization based on national characteristics. In a Synod of January 1749 Zinzendorf had firmly stated that 'The Brethren's Church . . . is a Corporation by itself (as the phrase is in England), and is like-wise the Inn of all those Children of God, who cannot otherwise subsist and come through the world'.[4] The *Acta Fratrum* meant for Zinzendorf that now his Tropus idea had the sanction of the State.

There was a widespread appreciation among the members of the Church of England that they could join a Congregation of the

[1] *Ibid.*, p. 181.   [2] *Ibid.*, p. 182.
[3] Cf. G. A. Wauer, *The Beginnings of the Brethren's Church in England* (London, 1901), p. 106: 'The Presbyterian Lords for once made common cause with the Anglicans on a religious question because the Brethren had Elders as well as Bishops.'
[4] *Acta Fratrum*, p. 92.

Unity of the Brethren without forfeiting their Anglican membership. When John Gambold, the young vicar of Stanton Harcourt, joined the Moravians in 1742 he informed the Bishop of Oxford that 'I mean to acknowledge my relation to the Established Church, to honour and serve her unconfined in a sort of free manner'. But, he went on, he must go 'where brethren dwell together in unity'. The Moravians were 'a happy people' and 'I longed to enjoy the blessings purchased by the blood of the Shepherd of our souls in fellowship with a little flock of His sheep who daily feed on the merits of His passion, and whose great concern is to build up one another in their most holy faith and to propagate the truth as it is in Jesus, for the good of others'.[1] Gambold was greatly attracted by the Tropus idea because it made possible the dual membership, and he was the first Englishman to state the case for an Anglican Tropus with any clarity in a letter to Zinzendorf in preparation for the London Synod in September 1749. Gambold pressed for the investment of an Anglican bishop as the head of the Tropus, and he suggested that until the right is granted to use the Book of Common Prayer regularly it might be adapted as a Moravian book of devotions. He then outlined a form of service for the Anglican Tropus which might be preceded by some such introduction as the following:

Inasmuch as we and some other nurslings of the Anglican Church, who have embraced the spiritual aid of the Moravian Brethren, yet certainly with no design, by so doing, of departing from our own proper religion; being however, in such a situation, it manifestly follows that we constitute an assembly which is extraordinary and extra-parochial, being *eclectically* made up out of various parishes; and that we, moreover, have a sacred place of meeting, which is certainly not a parish church; consequently many will immediately conclude that we have altogether forsaken the Anglican Church. Such, however, would be an erroneous opinion.

That we constitute such a society or assembly as we have mentioned, arises from our desire to exercise that salutary and vigorous discipline

---

[1] See my pamphlet, *John Gambold* (Moravian Book Room, London), p. 5, and Daniel Benham, *John Gambold* (London, 1865), p. 34.

which the Anglican Church pants for; but, by reason of its exceeding magnitude, cannot maintain; that we have a place in which we assemble, and a pulpit arises from our delight in hearing the principal doctrine respecting the grace of our Redeemer more clearly and more fully enunciated there, than can, in these times, be expected elsewhere; notwithstanding the same doctrine is maintained in the primary article of the Anglican Church.[1]

In the same letter Gambold argued that an Anglican Tropus might well 'with the greatest propriety' be recommended, 'inasmuch as it is beginning, as I imagine, to be thought desirable by the clergy of this country also'. Accordingly at the Synod of September 1749 it was agreed to offer the Presidency of the Anglican Tropus to Thomas Wilson, Bishop of Sodor and Man. He accepted the office with much joy.[2]

Although there was a campaign of literary abuse—a 'Battle of Books' as Hutton aptly calls it—conducted against the Moravians by the ignorant and the envious, the events of 1749 had given the Moravian Church a position of respect and influence in English church life. From 1749 to 1755 Zinzendorf virtually made his home in London, first in spacious quarters in Bloomsbury Square and then in Chelsea at Lindsey House, where the Pilgrim Congregation had its headquarters. It was in this great house that for six years the whole Moravian enterprise throughout the world had its centre. Zinzendorf received and visited the most eminent in Church and State.

Zinzendorf kept alive the hope for some more official union between the Anglican and Moravian Churches, and in February 1752 he wrote to Thomas Sherlock, Bishop of London, on behalf of the 'harmony of your Church and ours'. He suggested 'that a hearty intercourse of the worthiest prelates of your Church with our Foreman which will keep our mutual pastors in awe'; and that three chapels 'for our Church and two Tropuses' be erected in London.[3]

During this period, Moravian Settlements were established in

[1] Benham, *James Hutton*, p. 243–5.
[2] *Ibid.*, pp. 245–6.   [3] Addison, *op. cit.*, p. 189.

the North, West and Midlands of England and in Ireland, but every precaution was taken not to trespass on the territory of the other denominations. At Fetter Lane, for example, it was the custom to enter the members on the Congregation lists under the titles of the Tropuses from which they had come. 'When a brother comes into the Congregation', it was stated, 'from a Denomination he does not go into a new Church, but he retains his rights in the Denomination in which he was reared, and it remains for him an object of love and remembrance before the Lord. Should he be used outside of the Congregation in the service of his Church, he can still retain unharmed his privileges in the Congregation.' But still every encouragement was given to all would-be Moravian members to remain in or to return to the fold of the Church of England. 'When many of that pious people (i.e. Methodists) in England who left their Way', Zinzendorf told Archbishop Potter, 'appealed to me and the Brethren, I not only protested against receiving them among us, but endeavoured in the same time to recall them *home*.'[1] At a Synod held in Lindsey House in November 1754 it was agreed that the Moravian ecumenical witness should go forward in England and to the furtherance of that end an English bishop of the Moravians was elected. John Gambold was prevailed upon to accept this office and on 14 November 1754 he was consecrated by the Bishops de Watteville and Nitschmann.

As Ritschl observed, Zinzendorf 'did not succeed in laying the Moravian Church in the lap of the Anglicans';[2] but there continued to be an abundance of good will and fellowship between the two communions. For many years the members of the Anglican Tropus in the Moravian Congregations were led by the minister to take Holy Communion in the parish church. After such a visit, it was customary for the vicar and the Moravian minister to take a meal together, and that most amicably. When Gambold led a Moravian band of evangelists on a preaching tour in Wales, the Clerk of St David's publicly announced where the Brethren would lift up 'the word of faith'. Hannah More tells us that it was the Moravian minister, Benjamin La Trobe, who brought the great

[1] Addison, *op. cit.*, p. 181.   [2] Wauer, *op. cit.*, p. 107.

Dr Johnson 'to the renunciation of self and a simple reliance on Jesus as his Saviour'.[1] When Johnson was dying in 1784 he sent again and again for La Trobe who was out of town. As soon as the Moravian returned, he hurried to Bolt Court and assured the Doctor of the Christian consolations.

Perhaps above all it was in the field of missionary endeavours that the Moravians won the regard and support of the Anglicans: as we have seen, it was they who initiated that remarkable and ecumenical body called The London Association in aid of Moravian Missions. That the Moravians were keeping the world-mission of the Church constantly before the eyes of all Christians was generously recognized by the Anglicans. Dr William Brown wrote in 1814: 'The modesty of the Brethren, indeed, is so extreme, and their faith in God is so strong, that they do not come forward and make their wants known.' But the facts of their world-wide witness, the Doctor continued, 'require only to be stated, to induce many to come forward with their contributions to assist these extraordinary men in carrying on these noble and important undertakings in which they have been so long, so honourably and so successfully engaged'.[2]

A Splendid Failure

In 1749 Zinzendorf affirmed that seven Tropuses had been formed within the Congregation of God in the Spirit—Lutheran, Reformed, Moravian, Mennonite, Anglican, Neophytes (converts from among the heathen) and members of the Pilgrim Congregation. By 1789 any vestige of a claim to the continuance of the Tropuses had disappeared: from that year the heads of the respective Tropuses were no longer appointed. The vision of Zinzendorf was born out of time. It was too wide and tolerant; denominational mistrust and sectarian suspicion reduced it to a splendid failure. But in the opening up of avenues of fellowship between the

[1] W. Roberts, *Memoirs of the Life and Correspondence of Mrs H. More* (London, 1834), vol. i, pp. 377 f.
[2] *Moravian Messenger* (August, 1958), p. 24.

churches, in mutual discovery and intelligent awareness, in the emphasis on 'articles necessary to salvation' and in the toleration of differences in non-essentials, perhaps above all in the growing recognition of the rightful variety and full dimensions of the Church Universal, the vital principle of the Tropus idea is still calling us. We look forward to the advent of a commonwealth of Churches within one Church of Christ; and we salute the brave servant of the Lamb who tilled the soil for its foundation.

9

ECUMENICAL OUTWORKS

ZINZENDORF knew that co-operation could never be a substitute for unity. The question of Christian unity for him was always one of the heart. With reference to the ecumenical adventure he remarked in November 1748: 'The Tropus's have no reference at all to the heart. There is no difference in Christ Jesus: there is one Faith, one Saviour, one Merit, one Life and Happiness. The difference consists only in that manner of communicating ideas, wherein a person has been brought up.'[1] He knew full well that men could join in the same 'outward ceremonies and duties of religion, but in reality deny the truth of it'.[2]

But Zinzendorf did recognize that there were certain forms of co-operation—besides the fundamental missionary and evangelistic enterprises—which might usefully express and strengthen the innate unity of the 'christed ones' or true children of God. Here we may notice several of these representative 'Outworks' of ecumenism which Zinzendorf recognized and stimulated, and which still today form a part of the Moravian world-wide witness. It is partly because she has possessed these Outworks and because her servants of multi-racial origin have carried them into the international field that the Moravian Church has earned the character ascribed to her by Dr Martin Niemöller: 'The Moravian Church is an ecumenical microcosm.'

Worship and Music

To begin with, Zinzendorf was convinced that in the field of liturgical experiment and revision there lay a path to the recovery

[1] *Acta Fratrum*, p. 91.   [2] Berlin *Discourses*, p. 142.

of belief in and experience of the unity of the Church. He held a high conception of worship; he was averse to a rigidity of form, but he detested the slipshod. Worship was for him the purest and most effective address of man to God, and the purest and most effective evangelism towards man. He always related the rich liturgical life of the Moravians to service, *diakonia*. 'Herrnhut knew a diaconal liturgy.'[1] In his treatise on the *Rationale of the Brethren's Liturgies* Zinzendorf argued that when the liturgy is neglected and Divine Worship is 'stripped of all its outward decency' then 'the entire loss of Godliness itself' is the result.[2] Down to 1741 the Moravians used the Litany of Luther, but in that year Zinzendorf and Dober began work on a Litany which would still remain a bond of union with the Church historic and universal and yet express more particularly the spirit of their own Church. This 'Church Litany of the Brethren' set the Moravian worship in a clear ecumenical setting: the world-mission of the Church, for example, is emphasized in such a passage as this.

Keep our Doors open among the Heathen, and open those that are still shut;
Do not leave those Heathen desolate, from whom we are driven away; Have mercy on the Negroes, Savages, Slaves and Gypsies; Deliver the Ten Tribes of Israel from their blindness, rage and malice, and keep their Sealed ones.
Hear us, our dear Lord and God.[3]

In 1755 Zinzendorf published a *Liturgical Booklet,* and in 1757 a revised *Book of Litanies* which named and interceded for the churches of the world,[4] and prayed 'Unite the Children of God that are scattered abroad, and bring them once together from the Ends of the World'.[5] But again Zinzendorf allowed for the varying tem-

---

[1] Dr van der Linde, *op. cit.,* p. 423.   [2] *Acta Fratrum,* p. 93.   [3] *Ibid.,* p. 79.
[4] E.g., 'Under the Oriental Sees, Under the See of Rome, The Gallican and English Church, In all Evangelical and Reformed Churches, also in the East and West Indies, Under the See of Mark, And in all other Persuasions and Constitutions of Christendom, Even under the Spirit of Error and Concision' (*The Litany-Book,* 1759, p. 46).
[5] *Ibid.,* p. 46.

peraments and needs of the people at worship and he combined the formal and free emphases in the services of the Moravian Church.[1] And still today this legacy of Zinzendorf provides an ecumenical Outwork or 'bridge' across which the Christians of all the denominations may meet in mutual tolerance and recognition.

The Moravians had 'something to sing about', and they made a pioneering contribution to the development and spread of congregation-singing and music in the church life of the eighteenth century.[2] In England, they did much to break down the tyranny of the metrical psalms, the Old Version of Sternhold and Hopkins, and the foursquare tunes of Ravenscroft, Playford, Wilkins and Chetham. Indeed they did more: they extended the function and power of sacred song. It was more than a means of worship: it was a main factor in instruction, evangelism, comfort, warning, encouragement and church unity. Zinzendorf once said, 'There is more dogma in our canticles than in our prose.' In 1733 the Moravians declared: 'Our little children we instruct chiefly by hymns; whereby we find the most important truths most successfully insinuated into their minds.' Monsignor Knox has paid his tribute to the evangelistic influence of the singing Moravians. 'In our own literature', he writes, 'Moravianism will chiefly be remembered because our native enthusiasts have stolen its thunders. "Rock of Ages, cleft for me", is a work wholly Moravian in its inspiration; and it is difficult to imagine that either Wesleyanism or Evangelicalism could have taken so firm a hold on the religious sympathies of our fellow countrymen if pulpit eloquence had not been heralded and followed up by musical appeal.'[3]

Zinzendorf knew well the ecumenical power of hymn-singing

[1] It is recommended in the Moravian Church that a liturgy be used at least once a Sunday. A New Book of Liturgies has just been published by the British Moravian Church. 'In the liturgical form of its services the Unitas Fratrum gives expression to its union with the whole Church of Christ on earth, and as a living fellowship it will create ever new forms within the framework of its own tradition' (*Church Order of the Unitas Fratrum*, 1958, para. 101b).

[2] See Jenkins, *op. cit.*, p. 9; Knox, *op. cit.*, p. 404.

[3] *Op. cit.*, p. 404. For the Moravian influence on the Methodist hymn-singing, see Towlson, *op. cit.*, pp. 195 f.

and its contribution to the united witness of Christians of all traditions. It quickened the fellowship of the redeemed in the Congregations at home, in the mission stations abroad, and in the varied denominational gatherings of the Diaspora. Hymns and music were poured out and sung on every possible occasion, on land and sea, throughout the far stretches of the Moravian enterprise. No opportunity for singing was lost: even the harvesters had their own hymns and the night watchmen sang on their rounds. A hymn was frequently sung for each person at a conference; and verses were often composed on the spot to celebrate the return of a 'pilgrim' or the reception of a letter from the mission field. In particular, Zinzendorf loved the famous *Singstunde* or song-service which he himself had founded in Herrnhut. Many complete hymns were sung at such a service, and single stanzas were then chosen to continue a spontaneous theme as the evening advanced. Hymn-singing from memory was cultivated because only in this way, Zinzendorf argued, could the verses most effectively express the individual's experience.

Fortunately the Moravian love of singing was accompanied by an amazing literary and musical fertility. Every minister and missionary was expected to be able to turn a verse or start a chord, and many of the eighteenth century congregations have archives stored with odes and settings which, once used, were for the most part laid aside as the teeming imagination brought forth fresh compositions for the next celebration.

Zinzendorf made possible the publication of hymn books for use in Europe and America and on the mission fields; and they were remarkable in their conception and catholicity. *Das Gesangbuch der Gemeine in Herrnhuth* of 1735 was the parent hymn book of the Renewed Moravian Church. Its character and its contents influenced the *Collection of Hymns for Moravian Societies* published by James Hutton in London in 1741. In 1742 the first English Moravian Hymn Book, consisting of 187 hymns and 1,382 verses, appeared. This book, together with the Wesleyan Hymn Book of 1741 (also influenced by the *Gesangbuch* of 1735), were the first church hymnals in the English language. The first chronologically arranged collection of German hymns of all the ages, *Das Londoner Gesangbuch*, containing more than 3,000 hymns, came from Zinzendorf's private press at Lindsey House between 1753 and 1755.

As soon as they began their missionary adventure, the Moravians created the missionary hymn. From 1735 such hymns found their place in the hymn book, and Christian Gregor's great edition of 1778 contained a missionary section of eighty hymns written by thirty-six different authors.[1] Zinzendorf was determined that the converts on the mission fields should have their own collection of hymns in their own tongues, and in the course of time, and under the legacy of his inspiration, hymnals were produced for the Eskimos, the Negroes, the American Indians and the Creoles of Surinam. The story of Jacob Harvey, a Moravian Negro convert in Antigua, illustrates the infectious nature of the Moravian passion for hymnody. The missionary, finding Jacob's book crammed with slips of paper, blades of grass, dried leaves, cane-tops, and bits of rags, as book-marks, took him to task for damaging the volume. But Jacob exclaimed: 'O massa! Dem me partikler hymns.'

From the multitude of Moravian versifiers and in addition to the outstanding names of Zinzendorf, Spangenberg, Gregor, Gambold, Cennick, C. I. La Trobe, Swertner, Foster and James Montgomery, Julian's *Dictionary* enumerates forty-five Moravian hymn-writers of lesser importance[2]. Many of these writers were extremely young when their hymns began to appear. Some of them wrote hymns in German and in English. The *Was ist die lieblichste Figur* of L. E. Schlicht (1714–69) became as famous on the Continent as his 'What brought us together, what joined our hearts' became in England and America. It is to the credit of Zinzendorf and the Moravians that they were the first to give regular encouragement and recognition to women as hymn-writers. The German hymn book contained hymns by Anna Dober, Esther Grunbeck and over thirty each by Anna Nitschmann and the Countess Zinzendorf.[3] In the

[1] The earliest known missionary hymn in the English language was written by James Hutton for the Fetter Lane Congregation.

[2] P. 769.

[3] The Countess Zinzendorf wrote one of the most powerful of the Moravian missionary hymns (*Moravian Hymn Book*, No 473).

English book of 1742 we find the verses of Martha and Susannah Claggett, Dinah Raymond, Clare Taylor and Mary Stonehouse.

Together with their love of singing, Zinzendorf encouraged the Moravians in their love of music and gift for hymn-tune composition. A trombone ensemble or choir announced each significant private and public occasion: festivals, weddings, baptisms, pageants, funerals and the rising dawn service on Easter Sunday. Music was essential to the daily life and worship of the Moravians and wherever they went they formed an almost unrestricted musical outpost. When Benjamin Franklin visited the Moravians in the Pennsylvanian Settlement of Bethlehem in 1756 he recorded: 'I was at their Church, where I was entertained with good Musick, the Organ being accompanied with Violins, Hautboys, Flutes, Clarinets etc.' The Marquis de Chastellux entered the same town and he was 'astonished with the delicious sounds of an Italian concerto, but my surprise was still greater on entering the room where the performers turned out to be common workmen of different trades, playing for their amusement.'[1]

As much as in anything else, the tolerant and liberal outlook of Zinzendorf and the Moravians was reflected in their attitude to music. They regarded all music, with the exception of opera, as being important. They cherished orchestral and chamber music. From the earliest days in Herrnhut, informal gatherings of the people performed music for their own pleasure and enlightenment; and it was Spangenberg who gave the name of the *Collegium Musicum* to the musical sessions which developed from these gatherings. It is only in our own day that the pioneering and extensive contribution of the Moravian *Collegium Musicum*, particularly at Bethlehem and Salem, to the development of early American music is being realized afresh and explored.[2]

[1] D. M. McCorkle, *The Moravian Contribution to American Music* (Winston-Salem, N. Carolina, 1956), p. 4.

[2] See Donald M. McCorkle, *The Collegium Musicum Salem* (Winston-Salem, N. Carolina, 1956). The earliest known copy of Haydn's Symphony N. 17 in F Major was recently found in the Moravian archives at Winston-Salem. The first performance of Haydn's *Creation* in America was given by the Moravians in Bethlehem in 1811.

The first hymn tune-book used by the eighteenth century Moravians was the *Gesangbuch* of Freylinghausen, but they soon began to produce their own melodies and in 1736–7 their manuscript *Choralbuch* was issued in Herrnhut. It contained 200 tunes, arranged under 141 metres. Fifteen of these German tunes were included in John Wesley's first tune-book of 1742, *The Foundery Collection*, which contained forty-two tunes altogether.[1] Christian Gregor (1723–1801) and Christian Ignatius La Trobe (1758–1836) were the twin-Asaphs of the Moravian Church. Their tune-books set a lasting seal upon the church-music of the Moravians across the world. Both recognized the 'unity' conveyed by the universal language of music—a fact experienced most forcibly by La Trobe in his travels in South Africa where the Moravian Hottentots sang hymns to express their welcome to him. In 1759 Gregor began to arrange cantatas for the use of the Church, and from that time he poured out hymn tunes, anthems, sacred arias and canticles. He established the type of composition which found the widest favour with the Moravian musicians: a rather short anthem, generally in one movement, for chorus with instruments, a group of strings and the organ. La Trobe was born in Fulneck, Yorkshire, where his father was the minister and headmaster, and it was there, at a very early age, that 'the hymn-tunes and anthems of our Church . . . sunk with their solemn chords into my soul'.[2] Of Fulneck School, he writes:

Our dormitory was over the chapel; and I remember to this day, the delight with which I used to keep myself awake, to hear the congregation sing one of the Liturgies to the Father, Son and Spirit, always watching for that tune—Veni Sreator Cpiritus. I often thought, 'O how happy are those people! They are already in

[1] Cf. Towlson, *op. cit.*, p. 195: 'It was the sublime achievement of the Moravians that they introduced him (John Wesley), and through him thousands of his followers, to the beauty, the dignity, the reverence, the fitness of the German chorale, and to the personal and intimate song of the great Pietists.'

[2] C. I. La Trobe, *Letters to my Children*, written in 1815. (London, 1851), p. 28.

heaven, and I will live, to belong to those who are true followers of the Lamb.'[1]

Zinzendorf was quick to perceive and to encourage a gift for hymnody in others. He would often set a theme for the more promising writers. The results were shared, and new hymns were inspired. He himself was the 'master-singer' of the Moravian Church. He was never happier than when scribbling verses. Many of his hymns were *aus dem Herzen gesungen*, extemporized in the Moravian meetings as the need arose from the fullness of his heart and the fertility of his genius. 'Sometimes', wrote Bovet, 'he would sing a number of verses taken from various hymns, and interspersed with others, composed at the moment, thus producing a kind of lyric discourse—an echo to the voice of the Hebrew prophets— which seems to have produced a profound impression.'[2]

Zinzendorf wrote more than 2,000 hymns, the first at the age of twelve, and the last four days before his death. His hymns have a noble simplicity, directness and strength about them. They tell again and again of the redeeming Cross of Christ and his reconciling power, the utter devotion of the true Christian to Christ, and the reality and joy of the fellowship of all men in him. Zinzendorf is the singer of the ecumenical adventure, and still today his hymns are sung in over ninety languages. No man can sing 'O Thou to whose all-searching sight', 'O Spirit of grace', 'Jesus still lead on', 'The Saviour's blood and righteousness', 'My all in all, my Lord and Friend', 'Holy spotless Lamb of God', and 'Christian hearts in love united', without realizing again the glory and greatness of the Saviour who joins us all together, of every race and every land, in the one all-embracing fellowship of his love. In the glow of these verses we all cry out—

> Saviour, now for strength we plead,
> In Thy love together banded,
> To advance where Thou dost lead
> Doing what Thou hast commanded:

[1] *Ibid.*, p. 30. [2] *The Banished Count*, pp. 112–13.

Heart and hand we pledge Thee here,
Give us grace to persevere.[1]

It is a fair claim to make for Zinzendorf that he was the first ecumenical hymnologist. He saw the hymn book as a fundamental Outwork of Christian unity. As early as 1727 he essayed the remarkable feat of a Protestant sponsoring a hymnal and a prayer book for Roman Catholics. The book was composed of hymns which Zinzendorf regarded as belonging to the Church Universal and it was widely used by members of the Roman Church. In co-operation with John Gambold he published in London in 1754 *A Collection of Hymns of the Children of God in All Ages, from the Beginning till now*. This was the most comprehensive and ecumenical collection of hymns yet seen in Christendom, drawing from Roman Catholic, Protestant and Eastern sources. Indeed the Moravians sang from a larger collection of hymns and from more diverse sources than any body of Christians of the day, and as they sang their way around the world they broke down many walls of partition which blocked the ecumenical advance.

Lovefeasts

Perhaps of all the forms of Christian worship developed and encouraged by Zinzendorf, the re-discovered Lovefeast or *Agape* has proved the most virile in its ecumenical witness. After its revival in 1727,[2] the Lovefeast spread quickly throughout the whole Moravian enterprise. There was never any set form for this Service; and it still remains primarily a feast of singing, with an address appropriate to the occasion, accompanied by the serving of a simple meal. There were 'Festival' Lovefeasts for the Congregation and the Choirs and there were Lovefeasts for such celebrations as weddings and birthdays. Fundamentally the Lovefeasts express and quicken the fellowship of Christian believers through their fellowship with Christ. They invest 'the most solemn occasions

---

[1] *Moravian Hymn Book*, No 310.   [2] See p. 60 *supra*.

with the light of hope and sanctify the most joyous'.[1] At first rye-bread and water provided the meal; in England, the Brethren used wine and bread, but to prevent any confusion with the Lord's Supper, tea and a special bread or bun was introduced. Today in America, coffee, tea or lemonade is received. The spirit, rather than any special food, is what is distinctive.

It was often a Moravian Lovefeast which brought members of different denominations together in common worship for the first time. It is interesting to note that one of the sessions of the seventh Pennsylvanian Synod, June 1742, took the form of a Lovefeast on board the newly-arrived Moravian ship, the *Catharine*. In an open field at Great Gomersal, near Leeds, in 1742, a Lovefeast was held during which many people of various Christian traditions partook of the simple meal and listened to addresses by the Moravian, Spangenberg, and the Anglican, Benjamin Ingham. John Wesley soon realized the unifying power of the Lovefeasts and he intro-duced them to his people.[2] In a letter of 1805, the theologian Schleiermacher wrote of the Moravian Lovefeast: 'There is not throughout Christendom, in our day, a form of public worship which expresses more worthily, or awakens more thoroughly, the spirit of true Christian piety.'[3]

The Lovefeast has remained a vital bond of fellowship in the Moravian Church and it is now being considered by other denomi-nations as a possible ecumenical way of worship. Whilst 'the tables are fenced' it is not possible for the Holy Communion to be shared by all Christians as the true sacrament of unity; but the Lovefeast 'may yet prove to be the point at which the divided churches o Christendom may meet in a common act of worship and fellowship'.[4] A surprising acclamation has been given to a Lovefeast shared ir by Anglicans and Methodists in a country parish in Norfolk ir 1949;[5] but in Germany the Moravian Lovefeast has for many year

---

[1] See E. E. Gray and L. R. Gray, *Wilderness Christians*, p. 23.

[2] Towlson, *op. cit.*, p. 209.

[3] *Life and Letters* (E T by F. Rowan 1860), vol. ii, p. 23.

[4] *Intercommunion* (ed. D. Baillie and J. Marsh, London, 1952), p. 388.

[5] *Intercommunion, op. cit.*, p. 390.

given a centre of worship to the varying denominations.[1] In England, too, Anglican vicars and Free Church ministers have frequently—and in some places, regularly—shared in a Moravian Lovefeast; and in America, 'Christians of other Denominations are attracted to Moravian Lovefeasts in large numbers, and thus the spirit of fellowship and brotherhood is greatly advanced'.[2]

Education

Next, Zinzendorf welcomed Education as an 'Outwork' of Christian unity because it could express and help to form an ecumenical sensibility. As we have seen, he was an educative force of the first magnitude and he continued the valiant witness of the ancient Unitas Fratrum and of Comenius in particular to the vital grounding of education in religion. The unity of knowledge proceeds from a unifying faith. Fundamentally Zinzendorf recognized education as a unifying influence because its roots in all their reaches—in nature, in society and in the experience of life—are derived from the unity which all men share in Christ. As for Comenius, so for Zinzendorf, all discovery and achievement in knowledge is a further announcement of the presence of God; and all schools, no matter how wide and varied the curriculum, were for him a spiritual school of Christ. And education so conceived could form that centre of tolerance and mutual awareness which the divided Christendom of his day so desperately needed. At the

[1] The German Evangelical Kirchentag has included a 'Moravian Lovefeast'. The *Catholic Times* of 12 August 1960, reports: 'The Hofbrauhaus, Munich's famous beer cellar once used for Nazi rallies, was last week the scene of an ancient ceremony at which the Papal Nuncio, Cardinal Testa, helped to serve bread to about 600 people. The ceremony was an "agape", meal of Christian charity, revived on the Eucharistic" Day of charity and priesthood" for the first time in centuries. Cardinal Testa blessed the bread and wine. Then young priests served the wine while the Cardinal, assisted by several other Cardinals and Bishops, passed through the beer cellar, distributing bread to hundreds of church dignitaries and laymen. After everyone in the cellar had received bread and wine, the Cardinals and Bishops sat down for the common meal.'
[2] A. L. Fries, *Customs and Practices of the Moravian Church*, p. 59.

Danish court in 1731, Zinzendorf tells us, 'I broke out and informed the King that I would produce for him a university which could fill the whole world with the Gospel'.[1] For many years, in many places of the world, the Moravian school, attached to the congregation or mission station, was the only candle of the Lord in formal learning and instruction.

We cannot here enlarge upon the achievement which made Zinzendorf one of the pioneers of religious education.[2] It will be enough to illustrate his view of education as arising and ramifying from that fundamental unity which each soul enjoys in the Lamb of God. 'What, then, is child nurture?' Zinzendorf asks; 'it is a sacred, priestly method whereby souls are brought up from infancy so as not to think otherwise than that they belong to Christ and so the blessedness for them shall consist in knowing and serving him, and their greatest misfortune in becoming separated from him in any way whatsoever.'[3] 'Children', he wrote, 'cannot be too early acquainted with our Saviour and what He has done for us.' In his catechism for children, *The Pure Milk of the Doctrine of Jesus*, Zinzendorf is concerned not with implanting essential truths by tying them to verbal formulae, but with answering the question: 'How best can I lead a child to love and serve God, as He is presented in Christ?' The answer is to teach the child to centre his whole life in the Lamb; to enable the child to see Christ 'as clearly as a house', to dwell in his presence always and to confide in him at every moment. Zinzendorf called this 'walking with Jesus'; and, as Kinloch writes, 'it is not something purely otherworldly, it is a way of life which may be lived in the most concrete possible form. It embraces every conceivable activity, and is suffused with joy.'[4]

Zinzendorf would have nothing to do with the prevailing form of religious education which sought to mould all the children into the same pattern and to demand of them the same inward experi-

---

[1] *A History of the Ecumenical Movement*, p. 102.

[2] See T. F. Kinloch, *Pioneers of Religious Education*, ch. VII, and bibliography.

[3] See article by Professor John W. Fulton in the *Moravian* (Bethlehem, Pa.), vol. cv, No 5, pp. 13 f.

[4] *Op. cit.*, p. 83.

ences in a set progressive order. He recognized the manifoldness
of life and the individuality of the child. He opposed the tyranny
of schemes and methodism. As long as the child is 'walking with
Jesus' he is being nurtured in the best possible of all schools: 'In
Herrnhut we do not shape the children', he wrote; 'we leave that
to the Creator.' He was against coercive measures in any branch
of the child's education. The modern conception of 'teaching as
meeting' was implicit in his whole approach. In the Moravian
schools the teachers and pupils were accustomed to speak freely
with each other about the Christian faith, in a spirit of mutual
confidence and mutual interest. The teachers were required to be
able to 'enter into the children's feelings' and to understand 'how
to manage and interest them'; a vital feeling of delight in sheer
goodness and sound learning was always to be recognized and
encouraged. The teachers were 'called' to their tasks as a service
to the Lamb, and the pupils were taught to view their studies in the
same light; and this, Holmes said, gave 'to the educational system
of the Brethren its religious character—a character which is more
strikingly apparent in the principles and spirit inculcated on both
teachers and scholars, than in the regularity with which scriptural
instruction and devotional exercises are attended to in their
schools'.[1]

The variety of the subjects taught in the Moravian schools was
a wide and progressive one, and the spirit of free inquiry was not
discouraged.[2] On the pattern of the schools in Herrnhut, the
Moravian educational enterprise spread on the Continent, in
Great Britain and America. It was at the Moravian school in
Gnadenfrei that Schleiermacher, as he tells us, 'first became aware

[1] John Holmes, *History of the Protestant Church of the United Brethren*
(London, 1830), vol. ii, pp. 74 f.
[2] John Wesley remarked on the Moravian curriculum: 'In Herrnhut is
taught reading, writing, arithmetic, Latin, Greek, Hebrew, French, English,
history and geography' (*Journal*, vol. ii, pp. 50–51). See R. B. M. Hutton,
Through Two Centuries, An Account of the origin and growth of Fulneck
School, pp. 18 f., for evidence of the Moravian interest in science. Fulneck
School was founded in 1753 on a site in Yorkshire chosen by Zinzendorf;
James Montgomery, Richard Oastler, H. H. Asquith and Sir Robert Robin-
son, OM, are among its famous Old Boys.

of man's connection with a higher world. It was here that I developed that mystic faculty which I regard as essential'; and it was during his time at the Moravian school in Niesky that the same theologian learned to recognize the happiness of a life lived in the fellowship of Jesus Christ. He discovered too the just alliance which rightly exists between a living Christian faith and the spirit of free inquiry. 'My tutor', said Schleiermacher, 'urged me to inquire into the facts, and quietly think out conclusions for myself.'[1]

The liberal and progressive spirit which Zinzendorf inspired in Moravian education was quick to manifest itself in America. 'Many twentieth-century educational programmes', writes a modern American scholar, 'were inaugurated in eighteenth-century Moravian schools. Parent-teachers' meetings, community-school associations, educational and vocational guidance, and student participation in school management were common practices as early as 1750.'[2] The splendid historic recognition of the equal educational rights of boys and girls was exemplified in the boarding school for girls which Zinzendorf's daughter, the Countess Benigna, opened in the Ashmead House at Germantown, Pennsylvania, on 4 May 1742. During the American War of Independence, Bethlehem was visited by many eminent persons whose daughters were later entered at Benigna's school, then established in that city. Shortly after a visit by George Washington, his niece, the beautiful Eleanor Lee, became a pupil there. Such was the good fame and ecumenical character of the school that many of the daughters of the old Dutch families in New York, the German and Quaker families in Pennsylvania, and the English families of Virginia and the South, were most eager to be accepted as students. 'The education of children whose parents do not belong to our Church,' said the Moravians at a Synod, 'forms an important part of our usefulness. A wide field of blessed activity is thus opened to us, extending far beyond the limits of our own Church.' And indeed, children from all the denominations attended the Moravian schools (including Roman

[1] See A. J. Lewis, 'An Adventure in Education' in *Moravian Messenger* (London, May 1959), pp. 24–25.

[2] E. E. and L. R. Gray, *Wilderness Christians*, p. 331.

Catholics at Fulneck), but true to their ecumenical tradition, the Moravians made no attempt to proselytize or increase their own Church membership.[1]

Zinzendorf never regarded the Moravian educational enterprise as an adjunct to his mission of extending the 'fellowship of the Lamb' but as integral part of it. He regarded the manner in which the education of the children was carried out as one of the best evidences of the spiritual state of a Congregation. A wise and evangelical education, he argued, which respected the individuality of the child and at the same time weaned the child from the 'spiritual leprosy' of self-conceit, could nurture an informed as well as a consecrated apostolate and one which showed that 'uncommon tenderness for all sorts of souls, of what Persuasion soever'.[2]

Zinzendorf loved and reverenced children. He trained them not in conformity but in the right use of the special gifts which the Lamb had bestowed upon them. He frowned on dullness and monotony in the nurture of children, and in their own Choirs and services he offered them fields of expression fitted to their age and development. One of the special services which Zinzendorf encouraged for children in their search for light and colour was the *Christingle*. In recent years this peculiarly Moravian service has attracted increasing attention in other denominations, in the press and in broadcasting, and it might well form a permanent contribution to the ecumenical advance in worship.

For the origin of the *Christingle* Service we turn to the *Diary* of the Moravian Congregation at Marienborn, 20 December 1747. On that day John de Watteville conducted the children's service. It began with the singing of some hymn verses, some arranged to be sung antiphonally, two lines by the minister and two lines by the children. Then Watteville 'read over some sweet verses which some of the children had made on the little Lamb's birthday, and

---

[1] An excellent example of the Moravian self-effacement in their educational work is their handing over of their school at Wyke, Bradford, Yorks., to the vicar after a parish church had been built and he claimed the Moravian building as by established right!

[2] *Acta Fratrum*, p. 81.

made it quite lively and fresh to them what unspeakable happiness accrue to us from our Saviour's birth. . . . He has kindled in each happy little heart a flame which keeps ever burning to their joy and our happiness. For an impressive memorial of which each child shall now have a little, lighted wax-candle with a red ribbon which was done accordingly and occasioned in great and small, a happy children's joy.' Watteville concluded with the verse: 'Ah, my heart's lovely Jesus Christ, Kindle a pure flame, In each of these dear children's hearts, That theirs like Thine become.' Hereupon, the *Diary* concludes, 'the children went full of joy with their little lighted candles up to their rooms, and so went glad and happy to bed.' Wherever the Moravians went they took the *Christingle* Service: among the snows of Labrador, the wilderness of Pennsylvania, the heights of Tibet, the swamps of Surinam, the veldt of South Africa —throughout the world at Christmas time, the candles were lit and the children rejoiced. The symbols developed until today a *Christingle* consists of an orange, representing the world, with a candle inserted at its centre and lit to represent Christ the Light of the world, and two quills with nuts and currants impaled to represent the fruits of the world. The *Christingle* Service consists of carols and readings and towards the close of the service and during the singing of 'Morning Star, O cheering sight', the *Christingles* are carried round to the children. When all are served, the lights in the church are put out, and the children—holding high the illumined oranges—sing 'Silent Night, Holiest Night'.

Using the Bible

In Zinzendorf's 'liturgical method' of religious education the children sang and read their way into a close acquaintance with the life and work of the Lamb. The teacher expounded a passage from the Gospels and its meaning was illustrated and fixed in the memory by the singing of relevant verses from the hymn book.[1] 'To read the Bible is a blessing and a happiness,' wrote Zinzendorf. In it, 'the Saviour of Mankind in Person, after the most exact resem-

[1]See p. 164 *supra*.

blance' is to be found. 'The Bible is and remains,' he continued, 'our Rule *circa removenda* against which, and against the Spirit whereof, no one must dare to plead for anything.'[1] But Zinzendorf had no obscurantist view of the Scriptures; he was averse to any 'luxuriant novelty' in its interpretation; he was aware that much in the Scriptures had little interest for children and he arranged a shortened edition for them; and at Ebersdorf he produced at the Moravian press an edition of the Bible with prefaces and summaries at a price within the reach of the very poor. Further, as a contribution to the effective extension of the fellowship of Christ, Zinzendorf recognized the need for a translation of the Bible into the speech of the people in the idiom of their own day.[2] As Kinloch writes, 'over a hundred years before the Moffats and the Weizsackers began to turn the Bible into "modern speech" Zinzendorf had done the same thing'.[3]

Zinzendorf was quick to recognize that as we acknowledge in common the authority and constraint of the Word of God we are brought into a new measure of agreement with one another. But he was weary of the contemporary use of the Bible by many churchmen who made it principally a source of proof-texts for use in doctrinal disputes. He declared that one of the great unrecognized sins of his time was 'the preaching to death of souls with the dear Bible': the dulling insistence on the letter of the Scripture without any heartfelt understanding of the spirit. Out of his endeavour to lead the Brethren more deeply into the understanding

[1] *Acta Fratrum*, p. 90.

[2] Zinzendorf was a prodigious worker and translator: e.g., he translated the Gospels and the Acts on the outward voyage to St Thomas in 1738, and the Letters and Revelation on the return voyage. The Moravians did pioneering work in many native languages for the translation of the Bible. See *The Bible Translator*, vol. viii, no 4, p. 183, for the work of Schumann in Surinam; K. G. Hamilton, *John Ettwein*, pp. 109 f., for the Moravian interest in the native cultures and for Zeisberger's translations of the Bible into the Indian tongue; J. E. Hutton, *A History of Moravian Missions*, pp. 526 f., for the Moravian 'Dictionaries, Grammars, Translations and Works in Native Languages'. The first complete translation of the Bible into Estonian was made with Zinzendorf's aid (K. S. Latourette, *Christianity in a Revolutionary Age*, vol. ii, p. 198).

[3] *Op. cit.*, p. 81.

and the life of the Scriptures, Zinzendorf inaugurated one of the most widely used manuals of devotion of our own day—the Moravian *Text Book*. This has formed a devotional fellowship for over two centuries of Christians of all denominations all over the world. The custom of choosing a daily text or 'watchword' arose from the visits which were paid to each home every morning in Herrnhut following upon the great spiritual awakening of 13 August 1727. To provide a community of spiritual interest and emphasis, Zinzendorf provided the visitors with a verse of Scripture or a hymn stanza for each day of the week. The German word *Loosung* (now spelled *Losung*) used for the daily text signified among other things a signal agreed upon, countersign, watchword, password, and rallying cry. And so the 'watchword' came to be used by the Brethren as a password: it was studied as a guide to the life of each day, in prayer, in speech and in the various services. Still more, as Christian David wrote, 'we seek to know one another daily, through the Moravian Watchword, what manner of spirit we are, in order that we may know whether any one is friend or foe, whether he is of our mind or not, whether he is with us and striving consistently or against us'.

In 1730 the 'Watchwords' and 'Doctrinal Texts' were chosen for the whole year ensuing, and that custom has been maintained down to our own day. Two texts of Scripture and two hymn verses are used for each day. There are daily Bible readings set, Moravian festival days are noted, and prayer topics are suggested for regular periods. For over two hundred years the Text Book has preserved a close spiritual unity amongst all the Moravians scattered across the globe and it has formed a bond of peace and union amongst many thousands of Christians of all persuasions.[1]

---

[1] A few statistics may be mentioned here. 1,189,000 copies of the *Text Book* are printed for Germany, Austria and German-speaking Switzerland; 13,000 for French-speaking Switzerland and France; 7,658 for the United States, 3,000 for the British Isles and the West Indies, 37,000 for Denmark, 46,000 for Sweden, 127,500 for Finland, 3,500 for Czechoslovakia, 2,000 for Holland, 3,200 for Surinam and South Africa. There are also editions in Norwegian, in Estonian, in Polish, Hungarian, Ukrainian, and in the Spanish language for Central America. It is printed in thirteen European

Episcopacy

Lastly in this context we must consider briefly the Moravian episcopate. As we have seen, Zinzendorf continued for his and our own day the episcopal order of the ancient Unitas Fratrum. Freed from any particular or exclusive theory and regarding it simply as the historically developed means and symbol of the unity and continuity of the Christian Church, Zinzendorf welcomed episcopacy as an Outwork of the ecumenical advance.

At first it seems that Zinzendorf agreed to the revival or more correctly the continuation of the episcopacy of the ancient Unitas Fratrum on utilitarian grounds. True enough he was pressed by the Moravian-born members of Herrnhut to continue their old episcopal order, but the primary reason, as Bishop Hamilton points out, was the need to provide an uninterrupted supply of ordained ministers for the Mission fields.[1] The first Moravian missionaries were all laymen, and the Governments of the territories in which they worked soon objected to their administering the sacraments and solemnizing marriages among the native converts. Accordingly episcopacy was continued in the consecration of David Nitschmann in March 1735 'in order', as one contemporary document confirms, 'that such brethren could teach and carry out ecclesiastical rites in the colonies, who, however, shall in no other respects have preference or prestige in the Church'.[2] But this limitation of the office of the episcopate to 'the Moravian Church in foreign parts', as

---

languages, and in thirteen missionary languages. In South Africa it is printed in Afrikaans, Souto, Ovambo, Xosa and Sechwana; in Kinyamwesi for the Unyamwesi people; in Kishuaheli for the region of Lake Nyasa; in Eskimo for the people of Labrador; in Miskito for the Nicaragua Indians; for the Bush Negroes in Surinam; and in Chinese, Japanese and for the Kols in India.

The Moravian *Text Book* proved a powerful source of spiritual comfort and strength during the Second World War and in the vast disruption of life in Europe which followed. It was used in the prison camps, e.g. by Dietrich Bonhoeffer. See Prefaces to *Daily Texts of the Moravian Church* (Bethlehem, Pa., 1950 and 1961).

[1] In the article cited on p. 151 *supra*.   [2] *Loc. cit.*, p. 33.

Zinzendorf would have at first desired, was broken within a few months. The first ordination performed by Bishop Nitschmann was that of John George Waiblinger who was not destined for the mission field but for the pastorate of the projected Settlement of Pilgerruh in Schleswig. By 1745 episcopacy had become a recognized part of the Moravian witness wherever in the world the Moravian Church might be.

It must always be remembered that although the Brethren have preserved episcopacy through all the tribulations of their history— even when their Church seemed near to annihilation—they have never regarded the episcopate as being essential to a valid ordination and ministry. They have maintained their episcopal orders as belonging to the *bene esse* (well-being) of the Church, as expressing 'the most seemly manner', as a link with early Christianity and as a symbol of the Unitas Fratrum as an historically distinct branch of the great Church Universal. They have never allowed any theory of ordination to separate them from any body or ministry of Christians who call upon the name of the Lord Jesus in spirit and in truth. Never has their episcopate led the Brethren to question the validity of the ministry of the non-episcopal churches. They have maintained the view of Gregory in 1467 that the titles and forms of ordination are subordinate, that ministers are 'ordained and confirmed by our Lord Christ', and that they are called to service by the voice of the community either directly or through its chosen representatives.

Zinzendorf often reminded the Moravians that the Episcopal succession, however fitting and useful, was still only an outward form. 'Moravianism', he declared, 'does not consist in outward forms; ritual, creeds, constitutions, episcopal succession, apostolic deeds and martyrdoms may easily become objects of undue veneration.'[1] And again, he affirmed that 'if the episcopacy becomes a thing on the possession of which ministers and people pride themselves the Church is in danger of losing its apostolical character'.[2]

---

[1] F. F. Hagen, *Old Landmarks or Faith and Practice of the Moravian Church*, p. 74.

[2] *Ibid.*, p. 77.

Although during the lifetime of Zinzendorf there was some vagueness concerning the association of the bishops with administrative authority, it is quite clear that the Count was utterly opposed to any form or taint of prelacy. 'Should the Moravian Episcopacy', he wrote, 'ever degenerate into a Prelacy the Saviour will destroy it—whatever the Church may say or do to the contrary.'[1] He protested vigorously against the suggestion that Herrnhaag should be under the rule of the bishops and he annulled any steps to implement the suggestion which had been made during his absence in America. He stated firmly at the Synod of Ebersdorf in 1739 that 'our bishops are subordinate to the Elders, and have no functions except to ordain'. Gradually the conception of the bishop's office as a purely spiritual one was evolved and since Zinzendorf's time that conception has prevailed in the Moravian counsels. As Dr Guttery once remarked, 'the Moravians are the only Church to have accomplished the feat of retaining episcopacy without being ruled by bishops'.[2]

It was because the Episcopacy facilitated the ecumenical relationships of the Moravians with the other churches that Zinzendorf finally welcomed it. Particularly was this so in England. At the Synod of Lindheim in 1745, the Count told the members—'At that time (1737) I conferred with Archbishop Potter of Canterbury concerning the affairs of the Moravian Brethren. He said: "Although external matters are not too important, when one is concerned with souls, we should not neglect the episcopal succession, for a blessing rested on it." The present need for this Moravian episcopacy lies really in this: it has existed for nearly three hundred years, and one should not give up old, beneficial institutions; the cause of the Brethren especially in England has been helped by it. There we are considered an orthodox episcopal church.'[3]

Writing in 1755, Zinzendorf made clear the irenic character of the Moravian Church and also his own clear recognition of the

---

[1] *Loc. cit.*

[2] C. H. Shawe, *The Moravian Church and What It Stands For* (London, 1927), p. 14.

[3] Hamilton, *op. cit.*, p. 43.

authority of the bishops of any State-Church in whose territory the Moravians might be witnessing. 'Bishops of different Religions (i.e. Churches) cannot cross one another, because none can be deemed Diocesan but he of the National Belief. . . . The Ordinary of the Diocese of London (i.e. the Bishop of London) is considered by the Brethren as a Father, upon whom never any attempts will be made, to take the least advantage of supposed privileges in contradiction to his Regulations, or in defiance of his Authority. That is the true behaviour of a true Episcopal Church, which never sets up Altar against Altar.'[1] 'As they do not consider us a sectarian State Church', Zinzendorf told the Synod of Ebersdorf, the Socinians, Anabaptists and Quakers 'come in crowds to hear Leonard Dober and Barkhauser, and listen very reverently to their teachings. In London and Amsterdam, there are thousands who do not attend public worship; but if they attend our services but once, they hear something that will not allow them to stay away any longer.'

Moravians and Anglicans

Further light will be thrown upon the Moravian episcopacy as an ecumenical Outwork if we consider—in outline—the development of the relations between the Moravian Church and the Church of England since Zinzendorf's death. It was certainly traditional in the eighteenth century for the Anglicans to recognize the episcopate of the Unitas Fratrum.[2] The relation between the two communions was close and co-operative. Indeed it was the Moravian emphasis on the ethical and spiritual criteria of a valid ministry

[1] *An Exposition or True State* of the matters objected in England to the people known by the name of Unitas Fratrum, pt. i, p. 25; cf., James Hutton's comment in the *Additions* to *An Exposition*, p. 19. 'Though he (Zinzendorf) is a Bishop of another Constitution, he always looks upon the Bishop of London and his successors as on the nearest and most acceptable friends and directors of his conduct, if they please, when he is at London, and will scarce ever, I think, act in contradiction to his advice wilfully, when he shall be pleased to offer it.'

[2] See Norman Sykes, *William Wake*, vol. ii, pp. 7–8.

rather than any Anglican reluctance which prevented any episcopal partnership.[1]

The relationship between the Moravians and the Anglicans was brought into a new context by the Tractarian introduction of that particular theory of episcopacy which insists on the exclusive divine origin and apostolic succession of the episcopate as the only guarantee of valid sacraments—a view completely foreign to the Zinzendorfian position.[2] But long before the conversations between the Anglicans, Presbyterians and Methodists, so prominent in our own day, there were direct negotiations initiated by the Church of England for corporate union with the Moravian Church in Great Britain. Ever since 1878 these negotiations have continued, though not without intermission, and the Lambeth Conferences have debated and the Moravian Synods have listened to their Anglican Relations Committee, but still nothing concrete has been achieved. All these discussions have been centred mainly around the Moravian episcopacy: its historicity; its function in the Moravian Church; and its relation to the non-episcopal ministry in the Free Churches.

The question of the reciprocity in ministrations as between Anglicans and Moravians was brought before the Lambeth Conference of 1878 by Bishop Mitchinson of Barbados. Can a bishop

[1] From the *Diary* of the Moravian Settlement in Bethlehem, Pennsylvania (appendix to 11 November 1778), Bishop Hamilton has gleaned a most interesting incident and commentary on this point. A Lutheran, named Dr Kunze, a good friend of the Moravians, had suggested that Anglican candidates for holy orders, who were unable to proceed to England because of the American War of Independence, should be ordained by Moravian bishops in America. When the Moravian Bishop Ettwein heard that this idea was being discussed by certain members of the American Congress he begged his friend Henry Laurens to use his influence to prevent any such request being formally presented to the Church. Ettwein stated that twenty years previously the Bishop of London had proposed having Moravian bishops in America act for the Anglican Church in the ordination of their candidates. Moravians could not consent to this, said Ettwein, for 'a bishop of the Brethren's Church would count it a sin to ordain any man to such an office without possessing the assurance that the latter had personal faith in evangelical doctrines; he might even be an avowed deist!' *John Ettwein*, p. 89.

[2] See Norman Sykes, *Old Priest and New Presbyter* (Cambridge, 1958), *passim*.

of the Moravian Church be commissioned by an Anglican bishop to confirm or ordain on behalf of the Anglican Church? Can a bishop of the Anglican Church be commissioned by the Moravian Church to confirm or ordain on behalf of the Moravian Church? The Lambeth Conference of 1888 asked the Archbishop of Canterbury to appoint a Committee 'to examine into the history of Moravian Orders and the descent of their Episcopate'. In this committee, Dr Reichel (Bishop of Meath) held that there was a 'valid succession of the Moravian Episcopate', but Dr Stubbs (Bishop of Oxford) could not agree. In 1906 the Archbishop appointed a committee (including the Bishops of Salisbury, Birmingham, Rochester, Gloucester and Gibraltar) to make a thorough investigation of the succession of Moravian bishops. In the *Report* it was recognized that 'a succession of regularly constituted ministers has beyond question been maintained in that community from the year 1467 to the present time';[1] but 'the way to immediate intercommunion with the Unity as a Sister Church seems to be barred by the great uncertainty of its possessing the historic episcopate'.[2] The spirit of the negotiations was most tender and gracious and the Anglican bishops concluded: 'Certainly, in our opinion, no effort ought to be spared which might lead to full communion with a body so zealous in good works—especially in missions to the heathen—so charitable, modest, and unobtrusive in all its dealings with other Christian societies, and so large-minded in its relation to Christian truth, as the Unity whose principles were commended by Comenius to the guardianship of the Church of England.'[3] The Lambeth Conference of 1908 adopted a resolution which 'for the sake of unity, and as a particular expression of brotherly affection' provided for the participation of Anglican bishops in the consecration of bishops of the Unitas on certain conditions.[4] Bishop Hamilton Baynes, Assistant Bishop of Southwell, and Bishop Ethelbert Talbot of Central Pennsylvania, attended the Moravian Synod at

[1] *Report* of the Committee appointed by the Archbishop of Canterbury to consider the Orders of the Unitas Fratrum or Moravians (1907), p. 9.

[2] *Ibid.*, p. 62.   [3] *Ibid.*, p. 62.

[4] Details in *Report* of the Lambeth Conference, 1920, pp. 156 f.

Dukinfield, Cheshire, in 1908 and brought a greeting from the Archbishop of Canterbury, Dr Davidson:

Your bishops have come down in historical continuity through the first bishops, through Christ and the holy Apostles down to the present time. That is what we call the historical succession or historic episcopacy, and something which you hold as precious and as very sacred. We recognise that, and that is a very strong point of kinship and alliance already between you and us.[1]

And since 1908, following the spirit of the Archbishop's letter, the historic episcopate of the Moravians has been tacitly accepted by the Anglican bishops and priests except for those tied to the stiff and exclusive theory of episcopacy.[2]

After the 1913 report of the committee appointed by the 1908 Lambeth Conference, the Anglican-Moravian debate turned from the history to the present ordering of the Moravian ministry and its relevance to the function of the episcopate. 'It now appears', said the *Report* to the 1920 Lambeth Conference, 'that the Unitas permits deacons to celebrate Holy Communion, and also to administer Confirmation.'[3] In the conversations which followed, the Moravian Committee stated that, in certain circumstances, they would be 'prepared to recommend to our Provincial Synod that authority to confirm be given to Presbyters at their ordination'. This was in reply to the Anglican opinion that confirmation by presbyters might be permitted if authority to do so were directly delegated by bishops. Without denying the principle on which they had hitherto acted, 'for the sake of unity we are prepared to recommend to Synod that the celebration of the Holy Communion in the congregations be restricted to Bishops and Presbyters'.[4] But

[1] *A History of the Ecumenical Movement*, p. 295.
[2] An eminent Anglican, Sir Douglas L. Savory, has some interesting observations in *The Quarterly Review* (April 1957, pp. 156-7): 'But it does seem rather absurd that, while our Orders are definitely rejected by the Church of Rome, we should apply the same theory to the Moravians who have always maintained that they possess the Historic Episcopate.'
[3] *Report* of Lambeth Conference, p. 158.
[4] *Report* of Lambeth Conference (1930), p. 149.

the Anglicans replied in May 1921 that they could not accept a general delegation, given to presbyters at their ordination, of authority to confirm; such a delegation should be special for each occasion or conferred only to special presbyters. The Moravians replied in their Synod of 1922 that they considered their proposal concerning administration of confirmation by Presbyters adequate. The practice, they said, had precedents both in the Western and the Eastern Church, and was observed in other provinces of their Church from which they did not desire to be alienated.

The Moravians have remembered the broad tolerance of Zinzendorf and his view that in the Congregation of God in the Spirit there would be room for a variety of forms of ecclesiastical ordination and government—the episcopate, the council of presbyters and the congregation of the faithful. Accordingly they have conducted their negotiations with the Church of England in the light of a most tender regard for the non-episcopal churches. Indeed, as Addison points out, the most obvious practical difficulty in these negotiations has been the plainly expressed unwillingness of the Moravians 'to commit their Church to any concession in respect of Catholic order which would hinder their present fellowship and intercommunion with the Free Churches'.[1]

In the discussions following the Lambeth Conference of 1920 the Moravians were concerned to make clear that any alliance with the Anglican Communion should not be an absorption but a reunion; and that it should not imply in any way that we 'derive our status in this country from the Anglican Authorities'. They asserted again, in a resolution of their General Synod of 1909: 'We regard our position as that of an independent branch of the Church Catholic.'[2] On their part the Anglicans replied, 'The Church of England has no desire to lower the status of the Moravian Church, or take away its autonomy'.[3] But the Moravians were intent on clarifying the issue of their future relationship with the non-episcopal churches if the close 'alliance' with the Church of England came to pass:

[1] Addison, *op. cit.*, p. 152.
[2] *Documents on Christian Unity*, ed. G. K. A. Bell, 2nd ser., p. 118.
[3] *Ibid.*, p. 123.

'What we desire from you', they wrote to the Archbishop's Committee, 'is a more emphatic assurance that any existing relations which we possess and enjoy with Christian communities, with which we are already in inter-communion, would not be disturbed, and that the expression of that inter-communion should continue on our part to be quite free.' And again they referred to a Resolution of the Moravian General Synod of 1909: 'That we hold that Inter-communion with the Anglican Church must rest on the same mutual recognition and freedom to co-operate, as now exists between us and several Churches, Episcopal and others.' Another Resolution of the same Synod speaks of 'recognising the position of communicant members who have not been confirmed by a Bishop, or of communicant members of other Churches which do not observe' the rite of Confirmation.[1]

The Archbishop's Committee replied (December 1922) that 'we quite understand that a large individual liberty in these matters has been permitted' and that 'while we should be unwilling to lay down a stricter rule for the *Unitas Fratrum* than exists for Anglicans, we cannot advise our Moravian Brethren on being united with us to exercise Sacramental Communion with communities (other than the Foreign Provinces of the Unitas) which are not in recognised communion with the Church of England'.[2] The Moravian Committee could not accept this advice nor its implications. 'No restraint can be urged upon our members in this matter, nor can any adverse reflection be cast upon the exercise of such liberty. On the contrary, we wish it to be understood that this liberty may be used with the full cognizance of our church and that there is no taint of irregularity or undesirability attaching to it.' They went on, 'to us the special value of sacramental communion within our own spiritual household is not incompatible with availing oneself of the privileges of a guest or sharing as far as that is possible the joys and blessings of others not in immediate church connexion with us; and we feel that any disapproval or discouragement in this respect, whether implicit or explicit, public or private, implies an

[1] *Ibid.*, p. 126. [2] *Documents on Christian Unity* (2nd ser.), p. 131.

187

adverse judgement on the value of the ordinances of other communions and conduces to a spirit of aloofness and separation alien
to the character of our church and little calculated to further the
cause of Christian Union'.[1]

After 1924 the Anglican-Moravian negotiations lapsed, but
again in 1930 the Lambeth Conference requested the Archbishop
of Canterbury, Dr Lang, to appoint a committee to confer with
representatives of the Unitas Fratrum on relationships with the
Church of England. This Committee met, under the chairmanship of
the Bishop of Winchester, Dr Garbett, but in 1937 there was a
'mutual agreement to take no further action at present'.[2] In the
Report of the Lambeth Committee of 1948 on the Unity of the
Church it was stated: 'We note the fact that conversations with the
Moravian Church go back, though not without intermission, for a
long period. . . . The Committee appointed by the Archbishop of
Canterbury under the Chairmanship of the Bishop of Derby on
relations with the Free Churches has entered into communication
with the Moravians, and we recommend that negotiations should
be continued by that Committee.'[3]

But still no progress in any formal steps for union between
the Church of England and the Moravian Church has been made.
There is no likelihood of any advance in this matter until the Church
of England conception of 'Catholic' has been widened. As the
Moravian Bishop MacLeavy writes, 'Our ideas of Episcopal consecration and the Historic Episcopate do not coincide. Unless we are
wrong there must be a wider definition of the word "Catholic"
which will make room for non-Episcopal Churches whose Orders
are shown to be valid in the exercise of them.'[4] In particular, the
Moravians, like other Free Churchmen, find the idea of submission
to re-ordination by an Anglican bishop quite unacceptable. They
would heartily agree with the statement penned by Sir W. Robert-
son Nicoll in 1918: 'For a Free Church minister to submit to re-
ordination by a bishop, because the minister considers the act to be

[1] *Ibid.*, p. 137–8.   [2] *Documents on Christian Unity* (3rd ser.), p. 121.
[3] Sir Douglas Savory, *op. cit.*, p. 157.
[4] *Moravian Messenger* (February 1957), p. 4.

a harmless form, whereas the bishop himself holds it to be a most solemn and vital necessity, must appear to plain men as shockingly insincere.'[1]

Meanwhile the Moravian Church preserves its episcopate as an 'Outwork' of Christian unity. It has an episcopate as valid and as historic as the Anglican episcopate; it is free from any monarchical or exclusive pretensions; it is dedicated to a purely spiritual leadership. Its contribution to the unity of Christendom will grow more and more. Indeed, the Unitas Fratrum in its unique relation to the Free Churches has held episcopacy as a treasure in trust for them for centuries now. And its significance in this sphere is of more long-term importance than its significance to the life of the Moravian Church.

The First Genuine Ecumenicist

Here, then, is something more of the rich legacy of Zinzendorf's ecumenical vision: the Outworks or bridges which he attempted to build across the barriers of our separation to make possible both a spiritual and a practical traffic between the churches. And his vision still remains an exciting illumination of the principle of the Lund Conference of 1952 that the churches should 'act together in all matters except those in which deep differences of conviction compel them to act separately'.

But when all is said and done, we must return to the truth that the whole call to unity is a call to the Lamb of God in whom all unity is grounded. That from first to last was the inspiration and content of Zinzendorf's contribution to the ecumenical story. 'The Winding-up of all, the Result of our whole Preaching, and of all our Undertakings', the Moravians declared in a Synod of June 1748, 'is, that the People become tenderly enamoured with the Object of our Doctrine, Jesus Christ, and have such Intimacy and Confidence towards Him, that, with all their Misery and Defects, they can step directly before Him; and, when He has kissed, absolved, and blessed them, can afterwards, out of Love to their Beloved, in their

---

[1] T. H. Darlow, *Life and Letters*, p. 385.

Vocation, serve all their Fellow-Men as faithfully and sincerely, as if they did it all to our Lord Jesus Christ Himself.'[1] This is the unity, this is the life of heaven. It was no accident, says Karl Barth, that Zinzendorf, 'perhaps the only genuine Christocentric of the modern age', was 'the first genuine ecumenicist, i.e., the first really to speak and think wholly in terms of the matter itself'.[2]

[1] *Acta Fratrum*, p. 91.   [2] *Church Dogmatics*, vol. iv, pt. i, p. 683.

EPILOGUE

ZINZENDORF continued to live in London until 1755. He was as active as ever: visiting, preaching, writing and planning the global strategy of the Moravians. We catch a glimpse of his town life at Abington's coffee house where John Byrom was taken to see him in the company of some Quakers who had a great affection for the Count. 'And there was a room full of Germans and English', Byrom reported to his son, 'and before they parted Count Zinzendorf made a discourse upon a text in St Peter and some Germans gave it in English after every sentence, and I took out my book after a while and wrote what they said in shorthand, finding that they had no objection to it. . . . He is a good-natured, mild, loving-tempered man; he has been in all parts to raise up a spirit of Christianity amongst such as be ignorant of it.'[1] Zinzendorf would have liked that last phrase. He would have claimed no more for himself.

On 22 March 1755 Zinzendorf took his departure from London, after having had various important interviews with several men of rank, and at the same time enjoyed the pleasure of hearing their noble declarations respecting himself and the Moravian Church. During the last five years of his life which he spent at Herrnhut, he was troubled by the fever which lingered in him from the days of his Caribbean tour. But he did more, it was said, as a sick man than most men do when they are well. He spent many weeks in conference each year; he visited Holland and Switzerland; he drew up schemes for a renewal of the conversations with the Greeks and the Copts; and, eager to be of service on the missionary frontiers, he gave orders for a manor house to be built for him in Nazareth, Pennsylvania.

---

[1] *John Byrom*, ed. Henri Talon, p. 201.

In the early days of May 1760, a severe catarrhal fever took hold of him. He finished the manuscript for the 1761 Text Book and he composed an ode of thirty-six stanzas for the Single Sisters' Love-feast. As his illness grew worse, nearly a hundred brethren and sisters gathered in his bedroom. He turned to David Nitschmann and said: 'Did you suppose, in the beginning, that the Saviour would do as much as we now really see, in the various Moravian settlements, amongst the children of God of other Denominations, and amongst the heathen? I only entreated of him a few of the first-fruits of the latter, but there are now thousands of them. Nitschmann, what a formidable caravan from our Church already stands around the Lamb!'[1] Very early on the morning of 9 May he whispered to John de Watteville: 'Now, my dear son, I am going to the Saviour. I am ready. If he is no longer willing to use me here, I am quite ready to go to him.' He died that same day, just as Watteville was finishing the benediction—'and give thee peace'.

Zinzendorf was buried on 14 May. More than four thousand mourners were present. A company of imperial grenadiers was in attendance. The Congregation gathered in their Choirs; the sisters were dressed all in white; the trombones sounded; and the school children walked ahead, singing to the glory of the Lamb. Thirty-two ministers from the Moravian apostolate—from Holland, England, Ireland, North America, Greenland and Germany—took their turns to act as pallbearers. On the grave-stone these words were inscribed:

Here lie the remains of that unforgettable man of God, Nicolaus Ludwig Count and Lord of Zinzendorf and Pottendorf. Through God's grace and his own faithful and untiring service he became the honoured Ordinary of the Brethren's Unity, renewed in this eighteenth century. He was born at Dresden on May 26, 1700, and entered into the joy of his Lord on May 9, 1760. He was destined to bring forth fruit, fruit that should remain.

His fruit has remained. The Christian mission is world-wide.

[1] Spangenberg, *Zinzendorf*, p. 502.

Zinzendorf, 'that ecumenical theologian *avant la lettre*',[1] charted the ecumenical seas, and his map is still valid and directive for today. He contributed mightily to that change in the climate of Christendom which at long last is drawing the churches out of isolation into conference, out of mutual suspicion into mutual conversation and consolation. And his Moravians still remain to witness to his vision across the world:

The *Unitas Fratrum* or Unity of the Brethren do not, and will not, separate themselves from any child of God in any denomination of Christians; we will unfeignedly love and own as brethren all children of God, let them belong to whatever denomination they may.[2]

The Moravians 1760–1961

Inspired by his memory and by the undaunted traditions he had so powerfully planted in them, the Moravians continued Zinzendorf's world mission. The bases already established were strengthened and new ventures attempted. The missionaries renewed or firmly extended their work in Labrador (1770), South Africa (1792), Nicaragua (1849), Western Tibet (1853), Jerusalem (1867),[3] British Guiana (1878), the California mission to the North American Indians (1889), East Central Africa (Nyasa) (1891), East Central Africa (Unyamwezi) (1897), the Dominican Republic (1907),[4] and Honduras (1930).

Amidst all the vicissitudes to which an international Church is

[1] W. A. Visser 't Hooft, *The Pressure of our Common Calling* (London, 1959), pp. 27.

[2] From the introduction to the *Brotherly Agreement* which all full members of the Moravian Church in the eighteenth century had to sign. The wording differed from Congregation to Congregation but the content was essentially the same. See D. Benham, *Memoirs of James Hutton*, pp. 505 ff., and J. S. Groenfeldt, *Becoming a Member of the Moravian Church* (Bethlehem, Pa., 1954), p. 23 ff.

[3] The Moravian Leper Home, outside the walls of Jerusalem, has now been taken over by the Government of Israel. A new Moravian Home for Lepers was opened at Ramallah in Jordan on 12 June 1960.

[4] In 1960 this work was merged with the Evangelical Church of the Dominican Republic composed of Methodist, Presbyterian, Evangelical-United Brethren and Moravian churches.

heir—differences of nationalities, the wreck of oceanic and continental warfare, the difficulties of transport and communication, and the severest financial strains—the Moravian Church has remained a unity in spirit and in body. 'The Moravian Church', writes Dr Walser H. Allen, 'has never been divided. American, English, German, Czech, Dane, Dutch, West Indian, Eskimo, African, Tibetan, Bush Negro, Indian, or what have you, a Moravian is simply a Moravian.'[1] Out of countless examples of that unity of the spirit which has enabled the Brethren of different nations to overcome the threat of separation we may give here two instances. Soon after the First World War, Bishop S. H. Gapp tells us,[2] a British, a German and an American Moravian met on neutral ground at the Settlement in Zeist, Holland. They were to see whether the Moravian international Unity could survive the shock of War and the hatreds engendered by the bitter propaganda. The German was deeply depressed. He represented the vanquished; the other two, the victor. Would they be proud and unbrotherly? The three knew each other from earlier pre-War meetings. The American saw the disconsolate German. He hurried towards him, right hand extended, with a warm greeting upon his lips: 'O Brother,' mentioning his name. The German threw his arms around him and wept tears of joy. The three Moravians were soon at one in 'hearts united': the unity of the Brethren had survived. There came a moment at the Provincial Synod of the British Moravian Church held in London in the summer of 1946 when Bishop C. H. Shawe got up to read a letter he had received from the Board of the Moravian Church in Germany. The letter contained the most humble confession of guilt and of repentance for not doing more to resist the evil of the Nazi *régime*;[3] in the middle of the letter Bishop Shawe stopped reading and said, 'Brethren and Sisters, this is too much: all that the Lord requires of us to say to our German brethren is—"Come, here is our hand; take it in

[1] *The Moravians, A World-Wide Fellowship* (Bethlehem, Pa., 1940), p. 5.
[2] *Conference of Spiritual Descendants of John Hus* (Green Bay, Wisconsin), p. 5.
[3] In fact the Moravians did much and suffered much in their witness against the Nazi *régime*.

fellowship; and we will begin again, together." ' The Synod was deeply moved and the bond of unity was known to be unbreakable.

The organic international unity of the Moravian Church is as alive and as vivid as ever. No definitive constitution for the Church had been drawn up during Zinzendorf's lifetime, for in practice he was himself the final court of appeal. But after his death, it was finally decided in a series of Constitutional Synods (1760–75), presided over by Bishop Spangenberg, that a General Synod representative of all the Provinces should be the supreme legislative body of the Church; and that in inter-Synodal periods all supreme administrative authority should rest in a Unity's Elders' Conference (UEC) residing in Herrnhut. Until 1857 the world-wide Moravian Church was virtually governed from Herrnhut and few decisions could be taken in any of the Provinces without the consent of the UEC. But in that year, a General Synod granted Home Rule to the British and American Provinces with full powers to call their own Provincial Synods, to manage their own finances and property, and to make their own laws—subject to the final authority of General Synod. True to the principle that the Mission work was not the responsibility of any missionary society within the Moravian Church nor of any one Province, the Mission fields continued to be administered by a General Mission Board in Herrnhut on behalf of the whole Moravian Church.

The international character of the Moravian Church was effectively illustrated during the First World War when the Mission fields were cut off from the home base in Herrnhut: the British Moravians, for example, took over responsibility for the German work in East Central Africa, Labrador and Jerusalem; and the American Provinces assumed responsibility for the Moravian work in Central America and complete charge of the Alaskan field.[1]

[1] The respect accorded to the Moravians as an international body has been widespread. The American and French Governments gave a 'passport' of free passage to the Labrador ship going out from London during the American War of Independence (D. Benham, *Memoirs of James Hutton*, p. 515). During the First World War the U-boats were instructed not to harm the Moravian missionary ships; and not even Goebbels could stop the publication and circulation of the Moravian *Text Book* during the Second World War.

A General Synod was held in 1931, and another should have met in Herrnhut in 1941 but the World War made this impossible. At last it was with great joy that the General Synod assembled on 13 August 1957 at Bethlehem, Pennsylvania. There was a wide variety of peoples, of tongues and of backgrounds. There were advisory members and there were forty-four voting delegates representing the Moravian Church across the world. The assembly rose to its feet with cheering when Bishop Karel Reichel and Dr Radim Kalfus from Czechoslovakia entered the hall, for this Synod was also celebrating at the highest level the Quincentenary of the birth of the ancient Unitas Fratrum in Bohemia and Moravia.

This General Synod had two main aims: first, as Dr F. P. Stocker said at the opening service, to show before the world that, despite the years of struggle and poverty, of war and destruction since the last General Synod, 'the Moravian Unity is a living reality and that we are all one in Christ Jesus our Lord'; and together with this, to set forth the Moravian basic convictions concerning 'The Ground of the Unity' and its ecumenical outreach in a new statement of Doctrine to be sent to all the Congregations in every land. This purpose was wonderfully achieved. It may be summarized in one of the affirmations from *The Witness of the Unitas Fratrum*:

The Unitas Fratrum is committed to the unity of the children of God as a reality created by God in Jesus Christ. This unity has been granted and preserved within it as a Church formed out of various peoples, languages and denominations. Its very life, therefore, is to be of service to the Church Universal.[1]

The second task of the General Synod was to write into the *Church Order* of the Unitas Fratrum a recognition of the growing vitality and maturity of the younger branches of the Unity and of their just request to be allowed a fuller share in their own govern-

[1] *Church Order of the Unitas Fratrum (Moravian Church)*, published by order of the General Synod held at Bethlehem, Pennsylvania, 13 August–10 September 1957 (Bethlehem, Pa., 1958), ch. III, para. 150.

ment and in the deliberations of the General Synod as the supreme legislative body of the Church. Here was a situation which Zinzendorf had foreseen two centuries before and towards the solution of which he had pointed in his conception of a partnership of obedience in the unity and fellowship of Jesus Christ. The General Synod of 1957 faced this situation and welcomed it. In its decisions and in its new and modern Constitution for the Moravian Church, every encouragement was given to the younger branches together with a balancing emphasis on the need for experience and realized responsibility.

A significant and perhaps a momentous decision of the Synod was to abandon the old terms of 'home provinces' and 'mission fields' and to declare that henceforth all areas of the Unitas Fratrum shall be known as 'provinces'. Thus there are now in the worldwide Moravian Church three kinds of provinces: Associate, Synodal and Unity. An *Associate Province* (formerly called a mission field) is one not yet able to supply fully its own needs in men, money and leadership and finds help in these matters from the Unity as a whole or from some other Province which also provides a superintendent for the area. Each Associate Province is entitled to send one advisory member to the Unity Synod (the new name for the General Synod) which is to be convened every ten years. A *Synodal Province* is one which is deemed to be sufficiently developed to have its own Provincial Synod and to be able to a great extent to supply its own manpower and train its own leaders. The Chairman of its Provincial Board is the superintendent appointed by another province. It is entitled to send two voting delegates to the Unity Synod, one elected by its Provincial Board, and one by its Provincial Synod. A *Unity Province* is one which has developed its spiritual, material and human resources to the point at which it can assume full responsibility for its own life and work. It orders its own affairs and holds and administers its property independently. It supplies and sustains completely its own ministry irrespective of race or colour. When a province is first recognized by the Unity Synod as a Unity Province it is entitled to send three voting members to the Unity Synod; and when it is fully recognized, it has the right to send five delegates. And a Unity Province has the right independently to become a member of the World Council of Churches.[1]

All the provinces of the Moravian Church share in the common faith, tradition and witness of the Church, and the members of all the provinces are in brotherly relationship to one another. The classification of the Moravian Church into these provinces is an expression of the stature reached by each one in its growth towards maturity. The goal which is set before each province is that it shall strive to attain the fullness of Christian discipleship in its life, worship and organization. The provinces are linked together in a constitutional form of government which, while encouraging the liberty of provincial development, may provide mutual help and co-operation and provide the corporate responsibility of the Unity towards its provinces.[2]

To uphold and to further the development of the Unity and its ecumenical witness in all parts of the world in every way possible, the General Synod created a new executive authority known as the Unity Committee. Members of this Committee are elected by the Unity Synod, one each from the Provincial Boards of the Unity Provinces. This Committee is the vital link in administration, in information and in encouragement between all the Provinces of the Moravian Church in the periods intervening between one Unity Synod and another. Thus, although its membership does not exceed 330,000 in all its provinces, the Moravian Church is an alive and effective international unity maintaining the traditions inspired by Zinzendorf, seeking nothing for herself but welcoming

[1] The General Synod designated as *Unity Provinces*: the Czechoslovakian Province, the European Continental Province, the British Province, and the American Provinces, North and South. Provisions were made whereby South Africa, Western Province, after 1960, and Surinam, Jamaica and the East West Indies Provinces, after 1962, might advance from *Synodal* to Unity Provinces. Nicaragua was listed as a *Synodal Province*. Synod also agreed that South Africa, Eastern Province, after 1960, and the Southern Highlands Province, and the Unyamwezi Province, after 1962, should advance from *Associate* to Synodal Provinces whenever the conditions for a Synodal Province has been met. Labrador, Tibet, Alaska, and Honduras were designated as *Associate Provinces*.

[2] *Church Order of the Unitas Fratrum*, para. 201.

'every step that brings us nearer the goal of unity in Him' for all the children of God in all the denominations.[1] 'The episcopal seal of the *Unitas Fratrum*', said Dr Norman Sykes in a broadcast on the Quincentenary of the Church in 1957, 'bears the inscription: *Vicit Agnus noster eum sequamur*—"Our Lamb has conquered; let us follow Him." Throughout five centuries the Moravian Brethren have followed, thus contributing fully to the progress of the Gospel; and still by their efforts in various parts of the globe *Vexilla Regis prodeunt*, the royal banners forward go.'

To conclude. All great leaders in the Christian Church have been prophetic. They push back the boundaries of time and stand among us as our contemporaries. Such a man was Zinzendorf. He would have stood in the Assembly of the World Council of Churches in New Delhi 1961 as one who was quite at home. The matters discussed, he had discussed long ago. How happy he would have been—and without much surprise—to have greeted the Moravian delegates! Among them, there was Bishop S. U. Hastings from Jamaica and a native West Indian himself; Dr Heinz Renkewitz from the Continental Province; the Rev. Pierre Vittoz (once a missionary in Western Tibet) from the British Province; and the Rev. S. Kruger from the Western Province of South Africa, a new Unity Province of the Moravian Church and received at the Assembly into full membership of the World Council of Churches.

Perhaps too, in the light of the whole story of this book, we may find it most fitting that Dr Martin Neimöller should have brought the last Service of Worship of the Assembly to a close with the Moravian Watchword from the *Text Book* for the day (Tuesday, 5 December 1961):

> Turn mine eyes from looking at vanities;
> and give me life in thy ways (Ps. 119.37).

[1] *Ibid.*, para. 6.

SELECT BIBLIOGRAPHY

Zinzendorf, N. L.

Naturelle Reflexiones, 12 parts, 9 supplements (Ebersdorf, 1746–9)

Sixteen Discourses on the Redemption of Man by the Death of Christ, preached at Berlin (London, 1740)

Theologische Bedenken (Buedingen, 1742)

Nine Publick Discourses upon important Subjects in Religion, preached in Fetter Lane Chapel (London, 1748)

Acta Fratrum Unitatis in Anglia (London, 1749), many pieces from the hand of Zinzendorf

Maxims, Theological Ideas and Sentences (ed. John Gambold, London, 1751)

Peremptorisches Bedencken (London, 1753)

An Exposition, or True State of the Matters objected in England to the People known by the name of Unitas Fratrum (London, 1755)

Spangenberg, A. G.	*Leben des Herrn Nicolaus Ludwig Grafen und Herrn von Zinzendorf und Pottendorf,* 3 vols., (Barby, 1772–5). ET by Samuel Jackson in one volume, *The Life of Nicolas Lewis Count Zinzendorf* (London, 1838)
Benham, D.	*Memoirs of James Hutton* (London, 1856)
	The Memorial Days of the Renewed Church of the Brethren (London, 1895)
Wauer, G. A.	*The Beginnings of the Brethren's Church in England* (London, 1901)
Uttendörfer, O.	*Zinzendorf's Weltbetrachtung* (Berlin, 1929)
Addison, W. G.	*The Renewed Church of the United Brethren 1722–1930* (London, 1932)
Bettermann, W.	*Theologie und Sprache bei Zinzendorf* (Gotha, 1935)
Motel, H.	*Zinzendorf als ökumenischer Theologe* (Herrnhut, 1942)
Renkewitz, H.	*Zinzendorf* (Hamburg, 1948)
Sykes, N.	*Daniel Ernst Jablonski and the Church of England* (London, 1950)
Weinlick, J. R.	*Count Zinzendorf* (New York-Nashville, 1956)
Beyreuther, E.	*Der junge Zinzendorf* (Marburg, 1957)
Towlson, C. W.	*Moravian and Methodist* (London, 1957)
ed. Dodwell, C. R.	*The English Church and the Continent* (London, 1959)
Steinberg, H. G.	*Zinzendorf:* essays forming *Boeken der*
Schütz, H. L. C.	*Broeders* No I (Zeist, 1960)
Lutjeharms, W.	
Van der Linde, J. M.	

INDEX

Other Books on the Moravian Church

Freeman, Arthur J. *An Ecumenical Theology of the Heart: The Theology of Count Nicholas Ludwig von Zinzendorf.* Bethlehem, Pa., and Winston-Salem, N.C.: Moravian Church in America, 1998.

Fries, Adelaide L. *Customs and Practices of the Moravian Church.* Winston-Salem, N.C.: Board of Christian Education and Evangelism, 1973. 72 pp. $2.00.

Greenfield, John. *Power From On High.* Reprinted Bethlehem, Pa., and Winston-Salem, N.C.: Moravian Church in America, 1989. 96 pp. $4.00.

Hamilton, J. Taylor, and Kenneth G. Hamilton. *History of the Moravian Church.* Bethlehem, Pa., and Winston-Salem, N.C.: Interprovincial Board of Christian Education, 1967. 724 pp. $5.00.

Michel, Bernard E. *The Belfry that Moved.* Bethlehem, Pa.: Board of Christian Education and Evangelism, 1959. 64 pp., illustrated, for children. $.75.

Rican, Rudolf. *The History of the Unity of Brethren.* Translated by C. Daniel Crews. Bethlehem, Pa., and Winston-Salem, N.C.: Moravian Church in America, 1992. 442 pp. $22.00.

Sawyer, Edwin A. *All About the Moravians.* Bethlehem, Pa., and Winston-Salem, N.C.: Moravian Church in America, 1990. 80 pp. $6.00.

Schattschneider, Allen W. *Through Five Hundred Years.* Bethlehem, Pa., and Winston-Salem, N.C.: Moravian Church in America, 1956, rev. 1996. 148 pp., for youth, $5.00.

Weinlick, John R. *Count Zinzendorf.* Reprinted Bethlehem, Pa., and Winston-Salem, N.C.: Moravian Church in America, 1989. 240 pp. $10.00.

Weinlick, John R. and Albert H. Frank. *The Moravian Church through the Ages.* Bethlehem, Pa., and Winston-Salem, N.C.: Moravian Church in America, 1989. 128 pp. $8.00.

Available from:

Moravian Book and Gift Shop
614 S. Main St.
Winston-Salem, NC 27101
phone 336-723-6262 fax 336-723-8824

Board of Communications
P. O. Box 1245
Bethlehem , PA 18016-1245
phone 800-732-0591 fax 610-866-9223